Intimacy with God

Real Life Stories from *What Canst Thou Say?*

Other Books from *What Canst Thou Say:*

Gilpin, Mariellen, Editor, 2007. *Discovering God as Companion: Real Life Stories from What Canst Thou Say?* Bloomington, Indiana: AuthorHouse <authorhouse.com>.

Stensrude, Janice, Editor, 2014. *Proceedings of Sharing Our Stories: The First Annual Gathering of Friendly Mystics.* Raleigh NC: Lulu <lulu.com>.

Stensrude, Janice, Editor, 2015. *A Mystic Call . . . Naming the Spiritual Condition of the World: Proceedings of the Second Annual Gathering of Friendly Mystics.* Raleigh NC: Lulu <lulu.com>.

Intimacy with God

Real Life Stories from *What Canst Thou Say?*

Mariellen Gilpin, Earl Smith, and Judy Lumb, Editors

Front Cover: Photo by Anne Scherer

Copyright © 2015 What Canst Thou Say?
Published by *Producciones de la Hamaca*, Caye Caulker, Belize
<producciones-hamaca.com>

ISBN: 978-976-8142-634 (print)
ISBN: 978-976-8142-672 (e-book)

All rights reserved

No part of this book may be reproduced or transmitted in any form or by any means, graphic, electronic, or mechanical, including photocopying, recording, taping, or by any information storage retrieval system, without the written permission of the publisher.

The stories and poems in this collection were published in the newsletter *What Canst Thou Say*, and are reproduced here with permission. Biographical information reflects the date of original publication in *What Canst Thou Say*.

Cover photograph by Anne Scherer. Cover design by Judy Lumb.

Scripture quotations are from The ESV *Holy Bible, English Standard Version*, ©2001 Crossway, a publishing ministry of Good News Publishers. Used by permission. All rights reserved.

For information on this book or the publication *What Canst Thou Say?* contact: *What Canst Thou Say?* <whatcanstthousay.org>

c/o Michael Resman
815 9th StreetSW
Rochester MN 55902

Producciones de la Hamaca is dedicated to:
—Celebration and documentation of Earth and all her inhabitants,
—Restoration and conservation of Earth's natural resources,
—Creative expression of the sacredness of Earth and Spirit.

Contents

Preface ix
Intimacy with God: An Introduction 1
Getting Acquainted 3
  Roswitha Jarman *Where are you, Adam?* 4
  Merry Stanford *Spirit Birthing* 5
  Carmen Bruce *Gratitude* 7
  Charleen Krueger *A Sweet Scent* 8
  Mary R. Hopkins *My Search for Sophia* 9
  Dalton Roberts *Meeting God in a Honeysuckle Patch* 11

Intimacy with God in Nature 13
  Maurine Pyle *Getting Closer to God* 13
  Amy Perry *Seeing God by Seeing What Is* 14
  Lillian Heldreth *A Question of Respect* 15
  Gene Hillman *Eldered by a Dog* 16
  Linda Theresa *The Plea of an Old Dog* 17
  Helen Weaver Horn *Not My Own* 19
  Laurie Tucker *A Robin is Answered Prayer* 20
  Mary Waddington *The Vibrating Web of Connectedness* 21
  Hazel Jonjak *A Deer Shall Lead Thee* 23
  Lois Pomeroy *Wings of the Hen* 26
  David Blair *Animal Guides* 27
  Marcelle Martin *Hearing the Stones* 29
  Katharine Jacobsen *Lessons of the Spirit from the Earth Winds* 30
  Joyce Povolny *Silence Is the Holy Circle* 33
  Faith Paulsen *Star Dust* 34
  Glynis Lumb *The God of Wet Things* 35
  Christine O'Brien *A Friend of the Darkness* 37

A Committed Life 38
Michael Resman *A Full-Time Career* 39
Zarinea Lee Zolivea *Visualizing Harmony and Compatibility* 40
Elizabeth K. Gordon *Walk With Her* 41
Elizabeth De Sa *On Being Called* 45
Erin McDougall *Called on the Day of My Conception* 47
Judy Lumb *Collecting Parts of Myself* 49
Robin W. Harper *It's Just an Animal* 51
Kathleen Maia Tapp *Prayer of the World* 53
Phil Fitz *To Live God* 54
Peg Morton *A Spirit-Led Fast* 57
James Baker *Living in my Hands* 60
Maurine Pyle *Stretch Out Your Hands* 61
Rhonda Pfaltzgraff-Carlson *Prophecy Isn't Easy* 62

Finding God in Our Challenges 64
Mariellen Gilpin *God, It's You I Love* 65
Rosemary Blanchard *Like a Chick Pecking at Its Shell* 66
Jay Mittenthal *Undoing the Ego* 68
Eileen Bagus *Sensitivity: Asset or Problem?* 69
Marty (Verna) Neidigh *My Guardian Angel?* 71
Linda Caldwell Lee *Escape Plan* 73
Anne Highland *The Can Opener* 74
Pam Melick *Lifesaving Questions* 75
Mary Kay Glazer *Singing a New Song* 77
Heidi Blocher *A Moment of Light* 78
Jeanne Kimball *Facing Darkness as a Child of Light* 80
Viv Hawkins *Faith to Follow: Nothing to Fear* 82
Eric Sabelman *Stuck in a State of Prayer* 84
Barbara Clearbridge *As Real as Friendship* 85
Janis Ansell *Free and Infinite* 87
Janis Ansell *Q&A* 88
Jean Roberts *The Less I Said* 89
Ruth Stillwell *Easy Mover* 90
Faith Paulsen *The Blister* 91
Carol Roth *Out of the Blue* 94
Jennifer Frick *An Absolute Total Knowing* 96
Wendy Clarissa Geiger *A Vision of Sanity* 97

With God in Pain and Despair 99
Robin Arbiter *Promise and Pain; Lilith* 100
Robin Arbiter *OhSorrow, Here You Are* 100
Allison Randall *From Silence to Singing* 101
Lee Rada *From Addiction to Happiness* 103
Dalton Roberts *I Wonder What He Wrote in the Sand* 105
Carol Roth *Our Names Are Known* 106
Cathy Waisvisz *Legion's Healing* 110
Alicia Adams *The One Sent to Help* 111
Jaqueline Z. W. Hannah *Angel in a Trench Coat* 112
Angeline Reeks *Shadows* 114
Michael Resman *Hard Lessons* 115
Anne Highland *The Next Breath* 115
Lynn Kirby *Gratitude in the Face of ...* 117
Paul Schobernd *I'll Bring My Own Rocks* 118

Intimacy in the Journey with God 122
Beth Schobernd *Grace by the Sea* 123
Rhonda Pfaltzgraff-Carlson *An Encounter with the Comforter* ... 124
Carolyn Wilbur Treadway *Birthed into Grace* 126
Anne Scherer *Communication with God, with Spirit* 128
Deborah L. Shaw *Spirit Poured on Flesh* 129
Evelyn Miranda-Feliciano *Lord, Did You Also Wash Dishes?* ... 130
Mary Satterfield *One Thing I Have Asked of the Lord* 133
Rhonda Ashurst *Creating a Sacred Workplace* 134
Jennifer Elam *Dancing with God* 137
Charleen Krueger *Honey from the Sky* 138
Janet Ferguson *Does Evil Exist?* 139
Linda Theresa *When Does Grace Enter?* 140
Judith Favor *An Ineffable Presence* 141
Helen Siciliano *A Love I Could Not Put into Words* 142
Joyce B. Adams *Encounters with Jesus* 144
Hazel Jonjak *An All-Encompassing Affinity* 145
Marty (Verna) Neidigh *Invited Into the Kitchen* 146
William H. Mueller *The Beloved Disciple* 146
Diann Herzog *Walk as Children of Light* 148
Sadie Vernon *Dreams and Visions* 149
Marcia J. Jones *I Felt His Spirit Leave* 150
Lillian Heldreth *I Think Her Spirit Passed Then* 152

Celebrating Intimacy with God 153

- **Bob Barnes** *What Treasures!* 154
- **Patricia McBee** *To Love Thee More Dearly* 155
- **Jennifer Elam** *Sunrise on Easter Morning, 2011* 159
- **Helen Weaver Horn** *April Morning* 160
- **Sally Campbell** *Gifts Meant to Be Shared* 160
- **Zarinea Lee Zolivea** *Worshipful Vision* 162
- **James Baker** *As I Have Showed You* 163
- **Jennifer Elam** *Getting Real with God* 164
- **Christine O'Brien** *Blessings Beyond Naming* 165
- **Judy Lumb** *Ice in Someone Else's Soup* 165
- **Lauren Leach** *Bat Line to God* 166
- **Mariellen Gilpin** *Nooks and Crannies* 166
- **Mariellen Gilpin** *Horny for God* 167
- **Kathleen Maia Tapp** *Icon* 169
- **Kathleen Maia Tapp** *In the Land of the Great Mother* 170
- **Allison Randall** *Photography as Gratitude* 171
- **Patricia Reitemeyer** *My Golden Pond* 173
- **Michael Resman** *Worship* 174
- **Vera Dickinson** *Drenched with Love* 175
- **Janet Means Underhill** *I Give Thanks* 177
- **Janet Means Underhill** *Mystery and Wonder Fill My World* 178

Author Index 179
Past Issues of **What Canst Thou Say?** 180
In Memoriam 181

Preface

The stories in this book were first published in a journal, *What Canst Thou Say?* (WCTS). WCTS was begun in 1994 by Jean Roberts and Jim Flory to encourage sharing of mystical experience and contemplative practice among Quakers. They wrote, "It is like launching a kite: Jean and Jim will run down the beach to get it airborne, but lacking the breeze of your contributions of articles, responses, questions and quotes, it will not fly."

In the years since, Judith Detert-Moriarty, Jennifer Elam, Lissa Field, Mariellen Gilpin, Elizabeth K. Gordon, Lieselotte Heil, Richard Himmer, Chris Johns, Sue Kern, Linda Lee, Judy Lumb, Marcelle Martin, Patricia McBee, Grayce Mesner, Ellen Michaud, Roena Oesting, Amy Perry, Rhonda Pfaltzgraff-Carlson, Michael Resman, Carol Roth, Morgan Roth, Earl Smith, Kathleen Maia Tapp, Eleanor Warnock, Margaret Willits, and Wayne Yarnall have all helped to publish WCTS. Special thanks to all these volunteers and to all our readers and authors whose articles, responses, questions and quotes have given vitality to the ongoing publication of WCTS, adding the breeze to keep this kite afloat.

The story of this anthology begins ten years ago as we completed the anthology of the first ten years of WCTS, *Discovering God as Companion: Real Life Stories from What Canst Thou Say?*. After having communicated only by email, the editing of that volume and its launch allowed Mariellen Gilpin and Judy Lumb to meet in person for the first time. While we had learned to love one another electronically, the creativity that is engendered when we are all in the same room together is always a delight. What is truly inspiring to the WCTS editorial team is our ability to share leadership: We celebrate one another's spiritual gifts, contribute our own joyfully, and feel no need for hierarchy. God is our Editor-in-Chief, not one of us.

As part of that loving creativity, when Mike Resman first suggested WCTS sponsor an annual Gathering of Friendly Mystics, the other editors simply looked at one another and said, "Yeah!" Our first gathering in 2013 brought together 45 Quaker mystics for a weekend of "Sharing our Stories" — no business, no committees, just being together at Earlham College. That was followed in 2014 with the second annual gathering. As this anthology goes to press in 2015, we are eagerly looking forward to our third gathering, this time at Quaker Hill Conference Center in Richmond, Indiana.

Our WCTS gatherings have added Earl Smith and Rhonda Pfaltzgraff-Carlson to the WCTS editorial team, and Marcelle Martin and Diann Herzog to the WCTS gatherings team. Thanks for lending your creativity and spirituality to this work.

One of the challenges we faced in production of the anthology of the first ten years was getting permission from all the authors to reprint their articles, especially those who were deceased. It was quite an effort to track down family members. Following that, we changed our stated policy to "WCTS retains the right to publish initially and to reprint in WCTS anthologies," so we did not have to ask for permission to reprint in anthologies.

Likewise, it did not seem possible to update the biographical sketches for the author of each essay or poem. While it might seem strange to read outdated information, remember that was the condition of the author at that time. The date of publication appears right after the biographical sketches to remind us of when each contribution was written.

As a follow-up to *Discovering God as Companion*, the editors chose *Intimacy with God* as the theme for this celebration of the WCTS 20th anniversary. Focusing on intimacy with God seemed the natural consequence of our having "come out" together as Quaker mystics. We love the God of our experience, and God has richly blessed us, both as individuals and in this worship-sharing group in both print and electronic form, as well as in person in the annual gatherings.

Mariellen Gilpin and Earl Smith each lovingly read the entire ten years' worth of WCTS issues and selected their favorite articles and poems. Together they selected about 320 pages of articles and poems, and then Judy made up the rules by which we narrowed our volume to 190 pages: 1) We would use not more than three stories or poems by any one author; and 2) We wanted to represent all our regular authors with at least one story or poem.

Together we created tables of contents, putting all the selected articles into categories and in order. Judy Lumb prepared the layout, which we all reviewed and proofread until the volume was ready for Judy to shepherd through the publication process.

We thank Anne Scherer for submitting the beautiful cover photo just at the time Judy began to think about the cover. She saw Anne's photo and knew she had found the cover.

Mike Resman, Rhonda Pfaltzgraff-Carlson, and Patricia McBee read early drafts of this anthology and provided their insightful, indeed prophetic, comments and suggestions. Then all authors were given the next to final version to review and provided their wonderful endorsements and insights.

Mariellen Gilpin's husband John Gilpin's constancy in love has taught her what to expect of God, who first exhibited intimacy in relationships and taught us to hope and work for it in human relationships.

We thank God, our Editor-in-Chief, for the guidance, inspiration, and persistent humourful love, all provided in such abundance while we worked on this anthology. While God is the Editor-in-Chief, all the mistakes in transmission are ours.

Mariellen Gilpin, Earl Smith, and Judy Lumb, Editors

Intimacy with God: An Introduction

I lived in the same house with my father and ate at the same table with him. But I was taught not to think well of him. I needed a daddy, and God was my daddy. From early in my life, I prayed to a loving God, someone who heard my confidences and wanted me to be a good person. In high school, I listened to the minister thee-ing and thou-ing God and thought, "God is perfectly capable of understanding us when we speak in our own language, about our own concerns. God doesn't need us to put on airs with him." I wanted to be real with God.

In college, I turned to Quakerism because of the conviction that "Christ is come to lead his people himself." I took that as both challenge and reassurance. I went to silent worship most Sundays, knowing that each worship was different, depending on what I brought with me in my heart. I needed prayer, needed God, needed worship. I was on a quest for **intimacy**. *—Mariellen Gilpin*
(What Canst Thou Say, November 2009 "Bread and Roses")

When mystics want to talk about God, we have to speak in metaphor. We talk about God as the Cloud of Unknowing—we compare God the Unknowable to what we do know. Jesus compared God not to Father, the head of the household, but to the Person who cuddles us in his lap. When we love God with all our heart and mind and soul—when we have experienced mystic union with God—what better metaphors than those of married love? The language we turn to is the language of getting acquainted, courtship, the taking of vows, living our commitment to each other, in sickness and in health, for richer and poorer, taking joy in the ordinary, and weeping over losses. Yelling at God and praising God is all part of intimacy with our Beloved.

▶Intimacy with God

Jesus spoke of himself as the bridegroom. "And Jesus said unto them, 'Can the children of the bridechamber fast, while the bridegroom is with them? As long as they have the bridegroom with them, they cannot fast.'" (*Mark* 2:19)

St. Teresa of Avila says, "So mysterious is the secret and so sublime the favour that God thus bestows instantaneously on the soul, that it feels a supreme delight, only to be described by saying that our Lord vouchsafes for the moment to reveal to it His own heavenly glory in a far more subtle way than by any vision or spiritual delight. As far as can be understood, the soul, I mean the spirit of this soul, is made one with God, who is Himself a spirit, and Who has been pleased to show certain persons how far His Love for us extends in order that we may Praise His greatness. He has thus deigned to unite Himself to His creature: He has bound Himself to her as firmly as two human beings are joined in wedlock and will never separate Himself from her."[1]

This anthology, drawn from some of the sharings of authors who have written for *What Canst Thou Say?* during our second decade, seem to have fallen naturally into the stages of the life-journey. Jesus provided the wine at the wedding in Cana; the authors and editors of WCTS invite you to share in the ongoing marriage feast.

---

[1]*The Interior Castle* translated from the autograph of St. Teresa by the Benedictines of Stanbrook Abbey: London 1912, cap.ii.

Getting Acquainted

My beloved is like a gazelle or a young stag. Behold, there he stands behind our wall, gazing through the windows, looking through the lattice.
—Song of Solomon 2:9

When our Love peers at us through the lattice, we are both aroused and frightened: that lattice is our protection; we wove it ourselves. And yet... and yet...we long to be safe in our Lover's embrace. We peek through our lattice and hope.

We begin at the beginning with Adam and Eve as Roswitha Jarman ponders the purpose of her life; Merry Stanford feels called to give birth to her own soul; and Carmen Bruce births gratitude. Charleen Krueger smells the sweet scent of God, whom Mary Hopkins calls Sophia. Dalton Roberts meets God in a patch of wild honeysuckle.

Our authors invite you into a Love that cannot be put into words. Only metaphors will do.

Where are you, Adam?

Roswitha Jarman

Adam and Eve hid themselves in the garden of Eden after they had eaten of the fruit of the forbidden tree. Martin Buber, who tells this story in *The Way of Man*, explains, "Adam hides himself to avoid rendering account, to escape responsibility for his way of living. Every man hides for this purpose, for every man is Adam and finds himself in Adam's situation. To escape responsibility for his life, he turns existence into a system of hideouts." Adam stands for man or woman; I know this to be true of my life.

I need to hear this question and face it; I need to render account of my life. I need to take responsibility for myself, to understand where I am and what my purpose in life is in any place at any time.

I felt the power of this question recently as I sat in front of Fra Angelico's fresco of the Annunciation in the monastery of St. Marco in Florence. This wonderful fresco hangs just above the main staircase as you come up into the area of the monastic cells. I found a chair and pulled it up and did not mind the people as they came up the stairs. I knew I had to sit with this image. It is an Annunciation like many others, but I experienced a power pulling me deeper and deeper into the image. I believe Fra Angelico painted this Annunciation in a deeply prayerful moment. Prayer united the artist and me as I experienced the universal and timeless message depicted in this beautiful image.

This is not about the contested virginity of Mary, who is told by the angel that she will give birth in a miraculous way to the son of God. No, this Mary is you or me, man or woman, Christian or person of any faith or none, asked to lay aside our garments of ego and self importance so that we can hear and receive this powerful message: ***I am to give birth, we are to give birth to the Divine in our lives.***

In this fresco I saw Mary sitting in her chamber, her private place, leaning slightly forward in an intense listening mode; her arms gently folded in front of her. Her right hand—the hand of reason?—held gently by the left hand, the hand of compassion. Her blue outer garment—her personality in the world—softly slipped aside. She is looking past the angel to hear a voice far deeper in the space beyond. She hears that she is to be pregnant with the Divine and will give birth to the Divine; the seed within is complete.

I was overwhelmed as I understood this universal message; my body shook and I could not speak for some time.

Meister Eckhart speaks continually of our challenge to give birth to the Divine in our lives. We need to let go of all that gets in the way, all that clouds our hearing. We need to enter the deep stillness in humility and readiness.

When Eckhart was asked what this silent stillness is, he answered, "potential receptivity," and added, "It is in this that you will be perfected." Potential receptivity is a condition we can be in at any moment, and when we are open to it, the seed within us can come to life in us and through us in the world.

When asked, "How do I know that this birth has taken place in me?" He answers: "When everything tastes of God." If we could come into this state, where we taste (see and hear and feel) God in everything, would we not be filled with joy and with compassion for this our earth and all creation on it?

The challenge to live this experience in my life is ongoing. Too often my outer garment shields me from hearing the voice within; I go into hiding.

I pray that our contemplation may lead us to render account of our lives so that the seed within us can be touched by the Divine and become fertile and flow out in our lives wherever we are. Amen.

Roswitha Jarman, *York, England, walks to meeting along a small river. She always watches for a kingfisher, her bird of Divine presence, seldom seen. She rejoices at the wren that shows up instead; humble bird with a magnificent voice. Reading Meister Eckhard is inspirational for her. "I try to live prayer rather than say prayer, but I need constant reminding."*

(*What Canst Thou Say?* August 2010 "Questioning")

Spirit Birthing

Merry Stanford

Keeping my heart and soul open to the workings of the Spirit has taken exactly the kind of focus, courage and support as was required of me when I gave birth to my children. Both processes involved intense pain, and ended in an unmistakable sign of God's grace, giving great joy and hope.

When giving birth, I could not stop the process, though I did have some influence on how it went. I could slow it down, through my breathing practices—which was a very good thing in my case. I could even pretend things were not as they were—not such a good thing. With my second child, I pretended to myself that I wasn't as far along as I was, and so nearly arrived at the birthing place too late. But once the birthing process began, my babies did come. They had to come. I couldn't stop them from coming. I ultimately had no control over when and how they came, and in what shape they arrived. I only had control over myself: how I breathed, how I relaxed, how I rested when I could, how I used or didn't use medication, how I connected with those who were helping me, how open I was to the experience of being inwardly transformed by this birth.

The same has been true in my own spiritual birthing process. My early life was a horror of violence and deception, and I survived it by hiding the memories away, deep in my unconscious mind. When a part of one's experience is buried, a part of one's self gets buried with it. I lived most of my life only half alive. As an adult, attempting to respond to the inward promptings of a healing Spirit, I was led to a loving, inviting, gentle God—who lived in the innocent depths of my soul. In order to travel there, I have had to travel through some difficult memories. I have had to be willing to see what is there to see, to feel what is there to feel, to re-experience, accompanied, that which nearly destroyed me in isolation. There has been no other way to learn that I never lost, could never have lost, God's love.

I have had to learn how to keep open when I would rather have shut down in fear, or shut out in rage. I have had to learn to "go with the flow" of this spiritual birthing, breathing in and breathing out, letting go and letting God when the chaos was beyond me, taking hold and bearing up under it when I had the strength to do so. And because I had children for whom I was emotionally and financially responsible, I had to learn to do this around their needs. At those times when I couldn't manage it alone, I learned to call on God and people to help—to do the laundry, change the diaper, go to the grocery store, drive my children to school, hold me while I shook, or even just get me up in the morning.

I have had to be willing to experience all of myself—all my anger, loneliness, terror, despair—rather than to bury it in an inward tomb, or pretend it wasn't there. I had to be willing to work it like a pile of rotting compost, to dig it into the rich earth of my life. I found that I had to be willing to let others see the garbage, and discovered—to my great surprise—that there were many who responded in compassion and friendship. There have been several who watered that compost heap with their own tears, who took a hand at helping to turn it, who even added a little of their own material to help balance the mix and get it "cooking"!

I have persistently judged myself very harshly for having such a messy life on my hands—I wanted to heal without any tears, without despair, without fear. I believed that if God were walking with me, there wouldn't be so much pain, that I would be uplifted by God's presence, that I would be able to transcend the suffering, somehow smiling calmly through the storm that raged around me but didn't touch me.

It doesn't work that way in birthing children, nor do I think it works that way in spiritual birth. Pain touches us. It gets deep down into us and shakes us up, inside out, and all around. If we want to move forward, we have to find a way to breathe through it, to live with it. To open to it.

I don't think there is anything redemptive about pain. It is not beautiful, or holy, or a lesson that God sends us to refine our spirits. I don't think that suffering is necessary to our growth, nor that we have to suffer to know God. There are times when I find it absolutely blasphemous that the symbol of a whole faith is an instrument that was used to torture and kill, and that God has been blamed for willing the death! It is absolutely clear to me that God does not will suffering, nor cause it, nor control it.

And yet, in my life suffering has been transformative. It has also been, at times, harshly beautiful, in the way a winter field can be beautiful, clutched in the grips of a blizzard. It was suffering that catapulted me so resolutely toward God's healing presence. And there is a raw hope in me because a person called Jesus of Nazareth was able to be present to Love, even in the midst of an agonizing, humiliating death.

"Transcending" pain and suffering in the end is not something we can aim for, or use as a goal. It's not something we can accomplish through our effort. All we can really do is to stay open to the reality that we live in, a reality which includes plenty of suffering, and plenty of beauty.

It's through our open hearts that God creeps in, like a stowaway. It is our willingness to open that determines the kind of birth we will experience. God's Seed really does take root in the compost formed by working the soil of our Being. That Seed is our hope, and it will be born. It cannot be stopped. We have only to keep working the soil, stay open, and wait for the birthing day.

Merry Stanford *is a member of Red Cedar Friends Meeting in Lansing, Michigan. She travels with the FGC Traveling Ministries Program to assist meetings in healing and deepening their experience of the divine.*

(What Canst Thou Say? February 2006 "Touched by the Spirit")

Gratitude

Carmen Bruce

When I was a small girl, I knew Mystery. I knew Her as I sat in Silence in the embrace of the old weeping willow tree. I knew Her in my moonlit bedroom when the full moon's light and I communed. I knew Her as I smelled the purple lilacs and marveled at the beauty of the iris. I knew Her when I heard the whisper of the wind and watched the lightning dance across the steel-gray sky.

▶Intimacy with God

And then I lost Her ... my ... Mystery. I became socialized, conditioned, indoctrinated, inculcated into a world that seemed devoid of Her, until five years ago, the Sunday before Christmas. I found myself mysteriously sitting on a bench in a meetinghouse. In looking back, I knew Mystery led me to that bench. She sat with me in the silence among Friends.

Earlier this year, while walking, I met a professor who lived and taught at the seminary. He walked with Tillie, his four-legged companion, who effervesced with delight, playfulness, and spontaneity.

"She's a foundling," the professor said. "One of the seminarians found her, lost and abandoned, on the beltway." He then said the obvious, "She's very friendly."

"Do you think that is a quality of all foundlings?" I inquired.

"I think so," he responded reflectively, with a quiet certitude.

And again I knew it was Mystery who sat with the three of us on the side of the hill. I knew Her then; I know Her still. And I know today, as I knew from the start, of the gratitude in a foundling's heart. Amen.

Carmen Bruce *is a member of Providence (PA) Monthly Meeting. She lives as much as possible in the present moment, where she writes her poetry.*

(*What Canst Thou Say?* November 2007

"Feminine Aspects of the Divine")

A Sweet Scent

Charleen Krueger

Despite reading, meditating, holding people in the light, praying, and other daily spiritual practices, sometimes being led is like being poked with a sharp stick. "He leadeth me beside the still waters": my version usually reads "S/He drags me to the river and dunks my head until I surrender." But recently there has been a sweet scent summoning me in the right direction.

Before Christmas, at an inner city Meeting for Worship, I heard a man's footsteps as he entered, and with him came a whiff of frankincense and myrrh. When we introduced ourselves after meeting, he said he had been suddenly homeless, but he and his family were being sheltered by the Meeting.

On my way to visit a Meeting two hours from my home, I passed a man at the side of the road looking at a flat tire. I smelled frankincense and myrrh again. But the devil on my shoulder said "You'll be late for meeting!" Poke went the stick; I pulled over, and gave the man a can of stuff that inflates the tire and temporarily seals the leak.

Closer to the meeting, I stopped at a small store to check my directions. There was that smell again! I thought, "Now what?" in a not-too-kindly manner. Poke, poke. I looked around the parking lot and saw a woman looking at an obviously dry dipstick. I gave her two quarts of oil, and I wasn't even surprised I had it in my trunk. She told me I was a blessing. I told her we had both been blessed that day: she with oil, and I with frankincense and myrrh.

Charleen Krueger *is a member of Claremont Meeting, CA. Her bread job is nursing, but she is a knitter and designer. "We are knit together by our love of God and each other, reflecting God's love to each other and the world. "*

(What Canst Thou Say? August 2004 "Knowings")

My Search for Sophia

Mary Hopkins

I never missed Sunday School. It was Episcopalian. Something there gave me great happiness. Later, learning the Catechism and then going through the confirmation ceremony did nothing for me and so I became a seeker. The story of how I dove into Judaism and surfaced a Quaker must wait for another time. I sat in our little Quaker meeting, a woman in her thirties dedicated to meeting the needs of my four children, husband and parents. George Fox said that there is "That of God in every man." But suddenly it broke through to me that if there is That in every man, it must be in me too. I shook. My life changed.

Strong dreams haunted me as I explored my inner life. Before I went to sleep, I read of Goddesses: first the fifteen primordial Goddesses and then the thirteen fertile ones. I still remember the hair standing up on my neck as I read the description of Brigid. Perhaps it was then that I turned out the light and slept more soundly than I can remember before or after. Later I dreamed:

With strong emotion, I went into the Johnson Art Museum through the lower passage and into the basement. I was in a tiered room. I entered from the side and walked along a tier near the top. Above me, on a tier, sat my proud parents—happy in their expectation of my arrival. On the tiers below us were glass-topped tables in which their treasures were shown. The tables were made of cheap pine. I had a hard time walking past my parents on my right. My feelings for their treasures, below me on my left, were of contempt.

I approached a large door. I knew that I must go through it although I did not want to. It frightened me. When I pushed it open I was in a Great Hall—vaulted with beautiful muted violet and lavender paisley patterns slowly moving over the ceiling. Here was great meaning, not my parents' trinkets. Many wise women, white-haired, in black robes, were sitting around a U-shaped table. At the head of the room stood a great armored Viking holding a spear. The woman closest to me, on my right, gently smiled and said to me, "Welcome, we have been waiting for you," as she indicated the seat on the bench beside her.

In 1968, I read Elined Prys Kotschnig's "Womanhood in Myth and Life" published in the *Inward Light** and found myself deeply attracted to her description of Athena. In the midst of divorce proceedings and a rocky professional life, I was in a period of upheaval. The image of the strong woman, hand held high with a torch or spear, one foot firmly forward, gave me strength to deal with the difficult tasks of my life at that time.

I looked for pictures of the ancient Greek goddesses that form the matrix of archetypes that define women's journey, pictures of terracotta figurines of goddesses, queens, or women in daily life which date back many thousands of years. As I looked at them chronologically, the female experience seemed to fall away as the figures became square, not rounded; guarded not open; rigid, not realized. Some feminist theologians have wondered if the fall out of grace and into sin can be defined as the time when female qualities were eliminated from the godhead.

I began to realize what a female godhead would mean to my feelings about myself. Here was a soft, wise old woman who loved and nurtured me no matter what I did. Gone was the guilt, fear and distance of the male god. No demands were being made on me except to be my best self in relation to the world as it really is, with its dirty diapers, spilt milk, broken promises, dark and light.

It is important to recognize and honor the differences between male and female godheads. The male godhead is the father who orders life with law. The female godhead is the mother who loves unconditionally and intuits what is needed. It is possible to combine balanced law and order with unconditional love and nurture, and have all aspects of divinity flourish in society, if we attribute them evenly across the spectrum of gender.

Mary Hopkins *is a member of Kendal (PA) Monthly Meeting. She is the author and narrator of the videos* Woman and Her Symbols *and* Mother Earth: Revisioning the Sacred. *She uses images from art history to raise consciousness of women's spiritual history and sustenance.*

(What Canst Thou Say? November 2007

"Feminine Aspects of the Divine")

**Inward Light, Vol. XXXI, No. 74, Fall-Winter, 1968-9; and Vol XXXII, No. 75, Spring, 1969.*
(image) Restoration of the Venus of Lespugue, Musée de l'Homme, Paris

Meeting God In A Honeysuckle Patch
Dalton Roberts

From my earliest days, I had a desire to know God. Not the God I heard about in church, but a God who was Love. A lot of what I heard in church turned me off. I couldn't see God punishing anyone eternally or sending floods, or telling people to stone someone. The God I wanted to know was the one I saw calm the storm the night Mama prayed for me. I wanted to meet the one who shined at me in her eyes.

We had an evangelist called Uncle Bud Robinson who came about once a year to hold a revival. He was tongue-tied, but he sent out waves of love and humor when he talked. My sister, June, and I loved him. He talked about Jesus like he was his dearest and closest friend, and I think He was. Uncle Bud wrote a little booklet titled "A Pitcher of Cream" dedicated to a Jersey Cow. How can you not love a preacher like that?

Some evangelists who came specialized in terrifying people, as if you could scare people into the Kingdom of Love. I remember at altar call when Uncle Bud preached, people would swarm toward the altar at the end of his sermons, wanting to meet the dear Jesus that Uncle Bud had been talking about. I left the Nazarene Church when I got grown, but I will forever thank God for Uncle Bud.

I came to know God when Uncle Bud talked. And I came to know Him in a big growth of honeysuckle vines in the back of our property. When I was a young boy, I'd follow a rabbit trail back into the center of the vines and talk to God. I'm not saying God performed some kind of a miracle before my eyes to convince me He was real, but He did something much greater. He spoke Love to me. He became so real to me I felt I could reach out and touch him. He warmed my heart over and over, and that is the greatest miracle of all.

When I'd ask Him to help me be more kind and loving, He would do it. When I'd ask Him to give me strength, He'd do it. When there was turmoil in my family, I asked Him to help and He would. I came to know Him as "the Friend that sticketh closer than a brother" and many years later I wrote a song by that title. It's one of my songs that never fails to move me because it's all about the Friend I met in my honeysuckle cathedral.

Jesus said, "Unless you become as a little child, you can in no wise enter the Kingdom of Heaven." Some preacher might tell you that you have entered the Kingdom of Heaven, but I'll stick with the words of Jesus. Jesus was real smart. He was referring to a little child being trusting and open to the Truth. His heart is tender. He soaks up God like the dry earth soaks up a warm spring rain. I do understand that verse because I experienced it for myself when I was too young to let a wheel barrow load of questions make me doubt.

I remember a story about a little boy who ran in the house and told his mother he saw a lion in the yard. She told him to go to his room and ask the Lord to forgive him for telling a fib. When he came out she asked, "Did you tell the Lord you are sorry?" He said, "Yes, and He said it was OK because He thought it was a lion when he first saw it." If you want sweet laughs and to gain spiritual insights, ask children to talk about God. Some of it may be funny but it will also contain beauty that is untarnished by our adult filters.

No one except my mother ever asked me to describe my feelings and experiences about God. She always took the time to listen. She told of her experiences with God when she was a little girl and would go down to her spring and talk with God. She, too, felt it was one of the sources of her spiritual life. She likened the spring that bubbled up on their property to her inner spring that is deep inside all of us. She even told me one time that she didn't remember being born again, because she had always felt she and God were very close because of their talks beside the spring.

If we encouraged our children to enter into direct communication with God, maybe we would not have to preach to convert them. God would convert them. If children are converted in a honeysuckle cathedral, they are likely to begin a conversation with God that will continue the rest of their life.

I have had many agnostic and atheistic friends. They marvel at my simple feelings about God. The God I met listening to Uncle Bud and in my honeysuckle cathedral has been very real and satisfying to me all my life. I find that every day I live, this Friend is more real to me, and has anchored my life. Through all of my challenges and hard times, this Friend has remained inside, counseling and communing with me.

I cannot help believing in the Baptist doctrine of eternal security. Every time I have lost my way, He has come for me and carried me back to His fold on His shoulder. Believe me or not, I must testify to His faithfulness.

Dalton Roberts *is a singer, songwriter, columnist and former County Executive in Chattanooga, Tennessee. He enjoys Quaker and Unity services, and often performs in nursing homes and for other community groups. Reprinted with permission.*

(What Canst Thou Say? November 2012

"Children's Mystical Experiences"*)*

Intimacy with God in Nature

I was always mystical. From birth I recognized God in all of nature, especially when tree climbing. Sometimes I imagined that God was my magnolia tree that held me in her rocking arms. I loved to climb to the highest branches to get closer to God. I sure miss my tree climbing days. Now I dive deep into the silence and the womb of God instead of climbing higher. —Maurine Pyle
(What Canst Thou Say? November 2005 "God's Humor")

For many, the natural world outside our little wall and lattice beckons us toward God. Or is it that God invites us closer by leaving a trail through the natural world? Either way, or both, our authors learn to love God more by looking at Nature.

Maurine Pyle climbs a magnolia tree to get nearer to God; Amy Perry understands that seeing what is directly in front of us is to see God. Lillian Heldreth finds something holy in the ordinariness of pinto beans. A dog named Toby tells Gene Hillman his speaking in worship isn't spirit-led. Linda Theresa learns to let go and let God when her elderly dog Kelsie seeks one more adventure. Helen Weaver Horn reflects on Palestine as she plants her garden.

Several authors find their answers to life's questions by turning to animal guides: a robin provides an answer for Laurie Tucker; Mary Waddington connects with the turtle she rescues, and a deer provides the guidance Hazel Jonjak needs. For Lois Pomeroy, God is mother hen, while David Blair's guidance comes from several different animals.

Marcelle Martin hears God in the stones; Katharine Jacobsen recognizes that the winds of earth and water have a very similar mystery, rhythm, and pattern to that of the Holy Spirit. Joyce Povolny sings of holy silence; Faith Paulsen reminds us we are made of stardust; Glynis Lumb receives an urgent message in a vision of water deep in the earth; and Christine O'Brien tells us how the earth turns to darkness every day, dressing our lives in dark velvet and giving us rest.

Join our authors as they learn to walk with God by walking in Nature.

Intimacy with God
Seeing God by Seeing What Is
Amy Perry

One way I worship God is by using my camera to record what I see. It feels holy to notice what's there before me and then to honor it by framing it just right, holding the camera still, and pushing the button. This act creates a stillness and a release inside me.

When I capture what I see before me, I am honoring what is and honoring God, who created it and put it there before me. I honor God's creation by capturing the way it looked at that exact moment. (It may never look that way again!) When I honor what is, I am appreciating it exactly as it is. I am somehow participating in, somehow reflecting, the fact that God loves me and appreciates me exactly as I am.

When one is in the Now, one isn't concerned with the past or the future, so one has the ability to be aware of and connected to another dimension—the Eternal. Taking pictures enables me to preserve that particular Now.

Honoring what is enables me to somehow participate in the holiness, awesomeness and Otherness of God as conveyed by the Old Testament name for God: JHWH—I am that I am—the *is* of my subject and the *am* of God are connected.

Seeing what is; honoring what is, including who I am; knowing God loves me as I am; being in the now; preserving the Now that I have seen and delighted in—they are all related. I honor God's love for me and God's holiness by seeing and by using my camera to preserve what I see.

Amy Perry *is a member of First Friends Meeting, Indianapolis. She finds her photographic inspiration in the work of Thomas Merton.*

(What Canst Thou Say?
August 2005 "Seeing")

A Question of Respect

Lillian Heldreth

*I want to know how many women this morning
are cooking frijoles pintos,
soaking, parboiling, simmering over low heat for a long time
these painted seeds
my mother called
pinto beans.*

*And I want to know their real name.
not "beans, painted," as the Spaniards named them, but
what the Maya call them,
the ones who bred them from the wild,
who cooked them first,
served them re-cooked in oil,
with what the Hopi call piki bread,
and the Spaniards called "little turtles."*

*Quechua people, tell me, what do you call these beans
that I have loved for nearly seventy years?
I want to know their true name, so I can give thanks for them
with the respect they deserve.*

*So I can give thanks to your ancestors
for their great gift.*

Lillian Heldreth formerly attended Urbana-Champaign Meeting and is now a member of a Native American spirituality group in Marquette, Michigan, where she is writer/editor for the *Marquette Magazine*, a local tourist publication.

(*What Canst Thou Say?* February 2009 "Gratefulness")

Intimacy with God

Eldered by a Dog

Gene Hillman

Some twenty years ago Annapolis Friends were having a weekend retreat at Camp Catoctin in the Catoctin Mountains of Maryland. Most of us stayed in the surrounding shelters, but activities and meals were in the lodge. We had come with our families, and in two cases this included dogs. One was Noah, a border collie who was highly trained both as a guide dog and for field trials. The other was a young retriever named Toby, not trained for anything. Sunday morning we held worship in the lodge.

Both dogs lay next to their owners in front of the fire. Worship was deep. About halfway through the appointed time I felt led to speak. I forget the subject and what I said, but I remember that I stood and spoke what I was given. I spoke slowly as the words came to me. And the words did come, for about two and a half sentences, but then, halfway through that third sentence, the words stopped. I stood waiting but nothing came; I was done. Feeling this wasn't right, I finished the sentence on my own, and still on my own tried to sum up.

As soon as I started on my own, Toby stood up and looking directly at me (not really "pointing" me, but with a similar attitude), he started to bark in a regular cadence every second or two: "*ruff* ... *ruff* ... *ruff*..." I realized he had picked up on something so I stopped, and reluctantly sat back down. As soon as I stopped, Toby stopped too, lay back down and curled up where he had been, back to doing whatever it is dogs do in meeting for worship.

I have no way of knowing what he was sensing. Any change of tone or inflection would have been subtle, more subtle than what he hears in normal conversation. What did he pick up? I hesitate to say a dog's sense of the spiritual is that acute (does a dog have a soul?), although I am aware that, for example, some dogs can warn epileptics of seizures before they happen. As a skeptic who can look God in the face as did Moses and at the same time question His or Her reality, I look for rational explanations. But I now know Toby had somehow sensed when I had outrun my Guide, and was letting me know.

After Meeting Toby came up to me as I sat on a low wall in front of the lodge. I thanked him for his eldering as I tousled my elder's head and scratched him behind the ears.

*At the time **Gene Hillman** was a member of Annapolis Monthly Meeting in Baltimore Yearly Meeting. He is now a member of Middletown Monthly Meeting in Philadelphia Yearly Meeting.*

(What Canst Thou Say? May 2011 "Animals")

The Plea of an Old Dog

Linda Theresa

Blind and deaf, my dog Kelsie escaped the back yard. My health prohibited me from going after her. Chronic fatigue syndrome put me flat on my back most of the day. To walk twenty feet felt like willing dead legs to go just one more step…just one more step. Now my loving companion of 17 years roamed busy streets without a clue what was going on around her.

My calm reaction surprised me. Any other time there would have been a panic: worry and a sickening feeling of helplessness. Instead, I remained in a place of clarity and peace carried over from a lesson in love.

A few days before, I had dizzily gotten out of bed for my major outing of the day: hugging the wall on the way to the bathroom. As I sat on the toilet, my faithful companion joined me. White shadow, I called her, because ever since she was a puppy she clung to my side. Her hair bleached whiter as she got older, but she never lost her long eyelashes framing her large, dark brown eyes.

I groaned at the thought of petting Kelsie. Every movement used some of my nearly depleted energy supply, and cost me dearly. Anger swelled up. Kelsie had recently lost bladder control. You are so much work! I told her, And now you want pets too.

As I stared at her I couldn't help but soften. "All right, if this is the last thing I am able to do today, I give you what little energy I have." As I buried my fingers in the soft, curly hair of her back, time stood still. She turned, and our eyes locked in embrace. Without warning, I became her and she became me. I knew her more intimately than myself. For that moment in eternal time, I understood her and knew she had goals in life just as I did.

Then it was back to my aching muscles, and I inched my way back to my bed. However, that night I dreamed I was being loved unconditionally. The feeling was the same as between Kelsie and me, only God was loving the scared and helpless parts of me as if they were treasure.

Before, I thought of love as the strong desire to share your life with someone. Although my love had a caring quality, it also was possessive. I expected reciprocity and attention. But now, as I realized my beloved dog had run off, my first thoughts were, "Go for your goals, Kelsie. Live your life to its fullest!" It was a new kind of love.

I called friends and shelters trying to find my companion. When we were still unable to locate her the next day, I still could not make myself worry. Later that afternoon, I received a phone call. Some cheerleaders were preparing to practice next to the high school football field. They noticed a white patch in the middle of the field and went to remove it. There, curled into a little ball, was a dog. They presumed it was dead since it didn't move when they touched it. But when they shifted the collar to look at the tags, it opened its soft brown eyes.

A friend drove me to the high school, a few miles away. I wasn't strong enough to walk to the field, so I sat in the car and watched several girls huddling around a white mass. My friend knew Kelsie well, and I sighed with relief when Kelsie got up and limped along beside him.

Since she was nearly blind, Kelsie didn't recognize me until she came really close. Then she sprang into the air. She leaped and jumped. In the car, she bounded into my lap and couldn't stop licking my face. She had braved the wild, and come home for her last remaining days of life.

For a couple weeks after she died, every once in awhile I'd feel a loving energy in the room, and I knew Kelsie was checking up on me. She seemed so happy and ready for her next adventure. It was easy to let her go. In some mysterious way, I knew none of us ever really part.

Linda Theresa *gives thanks to the editors, staff, readers, contributors, and authors of WCTS. Reading and writing for WCTS is a joy.*

(What Canst Thou Say? August 2005 "Seeing")

Not My Own

Helen Weaver Horn

*I'm planting iris seed
around our swimming pond.
I crush each brittle pointed pod
shared by a friend, shaking
its bounty on the mud
and fallen leaves along the bank.
I come upon deer tracks,
and think how cloven hooves
will press these jet black seeds
deep into muck, embedding them
for winter as the slime does
quench their thirst.
I stand and bask in the reflection—
gold and russet trees on quiet water.
Deer will pause here just as I,
raise up their noses, dripping,
gaze, but always on alert,
ears cocked and nostrils
flared for scent of danger.
On the Palestinian West Bank
the danger is a way of life.
The soul who ventures out
into the open, needing food or
medicine, may well be shot.
Tanks rumble
through the ravaged streets,
their big guns sweeping.
Snipers, young recruits who follow
orders, hide around the corners,
wait. Our taxes arm them, help
their bullets fly. What privilege
have I to stand here gazing,
walk along this sheltered bank
to plant my flower seed?
This ground I cherish and invest
my life in is no more my own
than Hebron is Israeli
if a Palestinian elder like myself
can't walk into her orchard
now at harvest time,
can't pause to catch her breath
in peace and revel in the sheen
of light on glossy leaves
before she fills her basket
with the rich black olives
from her family's ancestral trees.*

Helen Weaver Horn is a member of Athens, Ohio, Meeting. She says of this poem, "I have been grateful when the Spirit has helped me channel my lamentation about American foreign policy and the violence in the world not just into lobby action and street protest, but poems that bring the realities home in concrete ways."

(*What Canst Thou Say?* February 2006 "Touched by the Spirit")

A Robin Is Answered Prayer
Laurie Tucker

One early summer day I was walking in my favorite park, a restored prairie near my home. As is my custom, I was praying as I walked, opening to the wisdom of the trees, to the beauty of the wildflowers, to the connectedness of the birds. I sought all that for myself that day, but sadness and fear kept me from receiving blessings from creation. As I walked I cried out to God, "Where are you today, my God? Are you here?"

God, in his infinite love and presence, answered me through a robin. As I walked through the wildflower garden, I saw a robin four feet off the path in the grass. I greeted him with a hello, as I always do. But this time, instead of hopping away from me, as usually happens, the robin hopped toward me. I stood still, and the robin came closer. I slowly knelt down, and the robin hopped closer still. Moving very slowly, I lay my open hand on the ground. The robin stopped right next to my hand. Scarcely breathing, I slowly and gently stroked the robin's back. It was silky and warm, impossibly soft. The robin shivered as I stroked, but held still.

I felt a deep connectedness to this being. No words were possible, but no words were necessary. Here was God's answer to my cries. We are all one; every part of God's creation knows and carries the presence of God. I felt such wonder, such awe, such joy, such gratitude. I was in the presence of God, and I felt it.

The sound of approaching footsteps broke the spell. The robin hopped back into the grass, still watching me. I bowed in deep gratitude for this show of love and trust. I continued my walk, uplifted and held. Thanks be to God for a robin!

Laurie Tucker *has grown beyond her Presbyterian roots. She has been blessed to meet many wise teachers along her way.*

(*What Canst Thou Say?* May 2011 "Animals")

The Vibrating Web of Connectedness

Mary Waddington

It was April, it was a Wednesday, and it was noon. The ritual of my sandwich making was encroached upon by an inward, persistent instruction that I eat my lunch out in the narrow back yard, which abuts the marsh. Totally uninviting. With only the hint of a lawn, that damp and insect-ridden space is always trying to become what it once was, tidal habitat. Furthermore, it held nothing to sit on. But I knew I should never argue with intuition.

Having found an empty crate, I flipped it upside down and sat among tufts of onion grass. My thoughts meandered until they were snared by a claw that scratched within the few evergreens bordering my house. I then heard a groan, a tragic rasp of a sigh that sounded both pinched and parched. Then another. I followed the sounds in a half-crouch, every muscle poised for flight. I parted juniper boughs and spotted my sunken window well. Peering into it, I saw why my intuition had called me to the back yard—a hapless turtle had been caught halfway into his fall and was wedged in a prison without bars. Empathy quickened and softened me. What is the taste of his fear? How intense is his longing for home? What does a slowly dehydrating body feel like? How many times has he clawed at the wall, hoping each time for a purchase and the promise of escape?

I had learned to identify only one species of turtle—the muddy and menacing snapper. Noting this turtle was not one, I reached for him. He quickly withdrew to his only protection and hid inside himself from the dread of not knowing. He stayed there while I pried him loose, and during this period of imposed intimacy we became friends.

I trudged toward the pond carrying the heaviness of Turtle sandwiched between my hands, one under and one over him. I did this to offer the only nourishment I had for him—the healing energy that flowed between my palms. My legs swished through last year's tall tawny field grass. I felt connected to the briars, the gnats, the damp, and especially to Turtle. My step suddenly became very light. There was great joy in our journey to the pond. It became the zenith of our bonding. We both had a history of having fallen into captivity, and we shared the experience of its accompanying fear and deprivation. My measured, light-footed stride became part of the celebration of our freedom, knowing well that freedom is a state one cannot truly comprehend or appreciate without having first gone through the agony of imprisonment.

At pond's edge I gave Turtle back, laying him ceremoniously at my feet. Before I had time to step out of his space, and with a speed that challenged his reputation, he thrust himself out of hiding and plunged into the life-giving waters. And in that instant I was quenched.

I quickly lost sight of Turtle and our link became a trail of sky-colored bubbles. Even after the last bubble burst the connection between us remained, and this tethered me to the rim of the pond. I stood there saturated by the fullness of an overwhelming gratitude. I felt the soft breeze as the unified breath of all souls who have struggled in bondage through all time. I felt it as a collective sigh from every being who persevered through their crying and kept the faith until freedom came. And then this soul breath within me blew upon embers of newfound compassion. It created a flame of prayer that leaped forth to all who are still in captivity. And within this fire was the heat of knowing that so long as even one of us remains in bondage, none of us is truly free.

Then it was Friday and it was yoga class. I sat next to my daughter Debbie, a sculptor who at that time lived and worked in a section of my house. The set of postures was over and we were sharing highlights of our week. Briefly, and for the very first time, I told my turtle story, aware as I spoke that astonishment was spreading over Debbie's face. When I finished, with trembling voice she shared her story:

For many days she had been unable to finish a commissioned sculpture that carried a pressing deadline. She had completed the upper half of this sculpture, which was a seated angel child. Yet for some reason she had not been able to sculpt an appropriate base for it, one that would meet the specified elevation and at the same time be worthy of the figure it supported. And then just two days ago, on Wednesday at lunchtime, the image of a turtle had flooded her mind. The energy from this image flowed down her arms, out through her fingers and into the pile of overworked clay beneath the angel, effortlessly transforming it into a free-spirited turtle. The circle sat in stunned silence, speechless. Two seemingly separate events had just been woven into one.

I rushed home to Debbie's studio yearning to witness something tangible from Wednesday's happening. I stood in reverence before her completed sculpture, feeling like I should be on my knees. There was my beloved Turtle, proudly carrying an angel on his back, obviously on a special mission. Debbie had not only captured his likeness but somehow his essence, which also felt like my essence. I found myself anchored to the spot by the same invisible cord that had tethered me to the rim of the pond.

For days I pondered this chain of events that began in my kitchen. A small but persistent nudge pushed me outdoors so I could hear a weak and raspy cry. Up to that point, Debbie's mind and the turtle's body had both been hopelessly stuck, perhaps for the same duration of time. While she clawed at her mound of unyielding clay he clawed at his wall, and neither could move forward. When I heard his cry for help was he hearing Debbie's? When I rescued him, was that the moment she was rescued?

I ponder still. In my search for answers I am given more questions: When do we realize that our lonely, silent struggle isolates and limits us? Where do we find the courage to ask for help? Why are we so often afraid to reach into that deep pocket of trust that holds the space for the humble call and the blessed response? Who makes the first move that vibrates the web of universal connectedness and awakens us to the presence of the other? I ease my questions into that place that is the Source of all questions and also the Repository for all answers.

Mary Waddington *is a member of Salem Meeting, New Jersey. Another story about her spiritual connection with animals appears in* Discovering God as Companion: Real Life Stories from What Canst Thou Say?

(What Canst Thou Say? August 2008 "Telepathy")

A Deer Shall Lead Thee

Hazel Jonyak

In the months leading to the US invasion of Iraq I vigiled with others in our small town. I placed throw rugs ("Persian" and American) on the icy parking lot, hung words of hope written on dishtowels and pillow cases on an old-fashioned drying rack, and held a blue and green earth flag my 85-year-old mother had sewed. My four-year-old grandson often stood with me, and when airplanes flew overhead my womb contracted with the fear of what planes over Baghdad would mean to Iraqi families. A double-vision of this reality (dark-windowed Suburbans and pickups whizzing by the Kwik-Stop across the street from our peace witness) and Near East reality (grandparents, mothers and fathers, children poised in fear of US power) forced me to express my heartache with the simplest and most utilitarian household materials: cloth, wood, and diaper pins.

When the attack on Iraq was announced, we gathered the next evening at our local Tree of Peace, an Arbor vitae, planted in ceremony by Jake Swamp of the Mohawk nation some twenty years ago. The flames from our candles and the songs of perseverance we sang couldn't comfort me or stop my crying.

I retreated to my lair, a one-room house in the woods. Near morning, from my dream world *I glimpsed a mother and child antelope pass by the window at the southeast corner of my home. They were a subdued reddish-brown, with the little one behind its mother, quietly continuing their journey toward a logging path to the west.*

With their brief presence in my world I was soothed. These exotic pronged antelope, kindred to our white-tailed deer (*waawaas-hkeshiwag*), gracefully entered our north woods radiating quiet centeredness. Then, at a thrift shop, I happened upon a four-inch pronged antelope created of paper and glue. It was red-orange, with touches of golden iridescence. I placed this kneeling antelope at the top of my bookcase, kitty-corner to my bed, to remind me of the peace and acceptance of the dream-visitors.

At about the time of the planting of the Tree of Peace twenty years ago, I had been scared in an encounter with a flesh and blood deer. My daughter and I had been driving to my brother's home at dusk. With no warning, a winter-starved doe ran into the side of our maroon Bronco. She was terribly hurt, unable to move, with two of her legs broken. As I placed my hand on her head and looked into her eyes, I was astounded that this deer which I had fatally injured communicated no fear or anger towards me. (Perhaps I had expected her to try to bite or get away from me, but it was more like an intimate connecting.) The deer had to be put down and there was no way I could do it.

A friend drove by, and stopped to put the deer out of its misery. We placed the body in the back of the Bronco and I drove on tremulously. My brother helped me gut the deer, and we found only twigs and bits of popple bark in her stomach. I took the carcass home and hung it outside to cool—but couldn't return to normal myself. In an awful enactment of Ojibwe sharing of my "first kill," I gave meat to friends and family, but could not bear to partake of the deer myself.

A couple of days later an Ojibwe elder came to visit. When I told him of the death of the deer, Bill told me I needed to put *asemaa* (tobacco) down to honor the spirit of the deer. After he left, I placed tobacco on the hide of the deer. Immediately I was comforted. The giving of tobacco placed the incident into the realm of the sacred—out of the grotesque. And with Bill's help later that spring I scraped and stretched the hide, noting how visceral and pungent life, death, and transforming-of-hide can be. (Bill had me soak the hide for three days so that the hair would slip off more easily!)

In my experience the antelope dream after the attack on Iraq and my killing of the deer (or the deer's offering her life to me) are connected. The antelope and deer brought an image or energy to smooth out my habitual agitated righteousness. The bombing of Iraq struck me especially hard, knowing that our Indo-European roots are shared with the ancient civilizations of the Near East, and that the United States was re-enacting barbaric ignorance and oil-lust against relatives. With my own killing-encounter of the most gentle of a gentle species, I, too, have shared the aggressor position, and was healed only with the grace of my counterpart, the deer.

With one last deer-car encounter, and death, I have now given up my car and driving. On November 14, my grandson and I were driving a car loaded with squash from my mother's garden. When we passed the tiny town of Birchwood, Wisconsin, a young forked buck came from the woods so quickly we didn't even see him until he was sliding up our hood to be tossed fifteen feet into the air. The buck hit a pickup coming from the opposite direction, and was dead when he hit the ground. I placed tobacco on his body and gave up my largest complicity in oil consumption.

Neither my grandson nor I were hurt, and now I walk the five miles to the college where I work sometimes, unless I catch a ride. (I'm not completely pure!) The little antelope remains on my bookshelf, and the deer I meet on my travels are no longer in danger from me. And when the US goes resource-grabbing, I don't feel personally implicated through lifestyle guilt.

Indinawemaganadag (all my relations).

Hazel Jonyak *attends Gathered Friends or Northern Meeting or FGC when possible. "I appreciate the Inner Light and receptive attitude and peace witness of Quaker practice. I also value sweat lodges and living in the woods for insights and guidance." She is non-native, was married to an Ojibwe man, and has a Polish-Ojibwe daughter and grandson.*

(*What Canst Thou Say?* May 2004 "Guidance")

Wings of the Hen

Lois Pomeroy

Little did we know—four post-retirement-age women friends visiting Hawaii—that we were about to come face to face with the Eternal Feminine, experiencing "that of God" in ourselves and in each other. As we relaxed on the front porch of the Honolulu Meeting House, we were suddenly energized by the arrival of a young Quaker mother who came bounding up the steps followed shyly by her adopted 7-year-old daughter. They were on holiday from the Big Island. "Come with us," she invited, "On my island you will see the beauty and power of God the Creator."

We couldn't refuse. Once there, we clambered down a muddy path into a caldera in Volcano National Park. Warm rain washed our faces and dripped from our ponchos, nurturing tiny plants springing up in every opening in the cool, gray lava. Mother Earth was actively giving birth to new life and hope; but there was also danger. In places the road had been covered by a gigantic cinder cone. Elsewhere it had dropped away completely, leaving only open sky beyond a sheer cliff. We were acutely aware of the molten lava just below our feet. Birth and death mixed together. Yet life predominated. Everywhere it was burgeoning with all the muck and mess that birth usually involves.

Later we picked out exotic goodies for lunch at the open air market, where smiling vendors greeted our guide with warmth and love. One used his machete to cut open green coconuts for us to drink from on the spot. Climbing into her rickety, old VW microbus we felt safe and nurtured. It was not so much like being in a womb (although something was growing and coming to life among us) as like being sheltered beneath the Wings of the Hen—words used in the New Testament to describe the mission of Jesus. All morning we explored and talked and laughed and shared, daring to be completely open with each other.

Our lunch stop brought us zigzagging steeply down into a narrow valley where a school had once been overwhelmed by a tidal wave. Lush vegetation had sprung up around the ruins and framed the memorial to the dead. Watching the breakers smash against the rocks with force even on this calm day, we relished our food and the fact that we were alive to eat it. The young daughter demonstrated hula movements to one of us who was just beginning to study that native art. As the two women moved—one young, one older—we watched in a kind of trance, sensing the spirit of the drowned children and their teachers. We were quieted by a sense that the two were dancing on holy ground.

A sense of the holy stayed with us for the rest of the day. Was it the power of place, the quality of the lives led by our two guides, the relationship growing amongst us? Perhaps it was all those things. Surely it was a gift to us from the two Quakers, both so nurturing and generous, both so tuned in to life's glories and pain. Today in my everyday life, I can sometimes get in touch again with the spirit of that day. When I am blessed, I can still see God in the remembered smile of the mother, in the body of the dancing daughter, in the faces of my friends and, even—can it be?—when I look at myself.

Lois Pomeroy *is a pastoral counselor and a member of New Paltz (New York) Meeting. She says, "Our Meeting is small but thriving with many children from babies to teens. We are, however, short on elders and would welcome visits from anyone so led."*

(*What Canst Thou Say?* November 2007
"Feminine Aspects of the Divine")

Animal Guides

David Blair

When I stand at the marsh below my house and look in the four directions, I remember the four animals who have appeared to me at important times and the messages they brought and still bring me.

At a very dark time in my life, fourteen years ago, I often heard and saw a pair of ravens flying above a hill to the east. I guess they were nesting there. I remembered that Raven flew into the dark to bring back fire to the First People, and so Raven taught me that light can be found in darkness if we have the courage to go into the dark. Raven has often appeared to remind me of this in the years since.

On another occasion, a large dark animal crossed the road in the distance, south of the marsh. A very big dog? Its hindquarters were too low. A black bear! By the time I reached the spot, the bear was gone. I followed its footprints and came to a huge boulder, left thousands of years ago by the glacier. I walked around the boulder and found a way up to the top, where I sat and meditated a while.

A few months later, I found my way to that boulder again. I had a painful choice to make and went there to meditate. As I did, a gentle rain fell, the sun shone through the rain and I cried, as I felt love and protection around me. My choice became clear. I chose well, turning away from a path that would have brought great pain and danger. I have always thanked Bear for taking me to that huge rock. Bear protected me.

Intimacy with God

The morning of my son's birth in 1979 I saw two otters in the water to the west of the place I stand. Otters are such joyful animals, totally comfortable on land and in the water, playful, faithful, smart. My son almost had Otter as his middle name! I have since seen otters there and in other places, and they always remind me that life can be lived with joy.

The hermit thrush's song is for me, as for Thoreau, the most beautiful and mysterious bird song. It beckons from deep in the woods to the north of the marsh, a distant music. A story I treasure tells of the hermit thrush who was brave enough, of all the animals, to come to earth to help a little girl named Sylvia who was lost and despairing. She'd forgotten that she was born from God and loved by God. The hermit thrush's song reminded her of this, and though the thrush could not stay on earth to be with her, its song remained with her always, and she never forgot. So the hermit thrush reminds me that God loves me.

Raven and courage in the east; Bear and protection in the south; Otter and joy in the west; Hermit Thrush and God's love in the north. These are my companions not only when I stand at the marsh, but any place I am in the world as I face the four directions.

David Blair has lived and worked in China, the Philippines and Vietnam. His inner journey has taken him to even more amazing places. David now directs the Mariposa Museum and World Culture Center in Peterborough, NH, a museum that brings the world to New England's doorstep in service of a peaceful and connected world: www.mariposamuseum.org.

(*What Canst Thou Say?* May 2011 "Animals")

Hearing the Stones
Marcelle Martin

One day I heard the stones
speaking to me.
Over four seasons I had been
walking the same path
through the woods, up the hill to the pond,
from summer to fall to winter to spring.
My mind had become calm
better able to reflect
the wide blue sky, the heavens,
able to listen and receive.
Now as I came down the trail
I could hear a low, steady singing
a humming, a vibrating.
I awakened to the cliff-like walls of stones
I'd passed day by day
their layers visible as ridges, gray,
spotted with lichen and moss.
All along they had been communicating to me
teaching me solidity,
stability
endurance to remain
and hold fast
over long ages
amid many changes
silent, solid, peaceful.

Marcelle Martin, a member of Chestnut Hill Meeting (PA) is the author of the Pendle Hill pamphlet, *Invitation to a Deeper Communion*.

(*What Canst Thou Say?* May 2004 "Guidance")

Lessons of the Spirit from the Earth Winds

Katharine Jacobsen

Childhood? Yes, certainly, but with lifetime impact. "Mystical?" Yes, if the word is taken to mean the living connection between the tangible, physical world and Something beyond. "Experience?" Yes, but not one experience, many. But let me begin at the beginning.

My father was forty-four when I was born, the first of his three daughters. At the top of a list of things for which he was admired by many who lived on our small Wisconsin lake, "Uncle Elmer" was considered a remarkable sailboat skipper. He could anticipate the wind and position his boat accordingly, ready to get the most out of every gust. In the sailors' vernacular, he knew how "to climb the wind." Climbing the wind is how a sailboat reaches its destination as quickly and surely as possible.

Because he could anticipate wind changes, a continuing reality on inland lakes not far from the prairies, my dad was a legendary competitor in the weekend sailing races on our lake and beyond. "Watch what's happening like a cat ready to pounce," he would tell his crew at strategic times, such as, crossing the starting line to windward of other boats and rounding the buoys with only inches to spare. His sailboat, the "Me Too," finished first in the races more often than not.

The year I became old enough to race a beginners' racing boat with a crew member of whatever age and experience was called for, my birthday in May was blessed by a third-hand, wooden Cub Boat called the "Lollypop," and at race time each Saturday morning, my father scrunched his not slender, midlife frame into the front of the cockpit, where he could hold the jib sheet, watch for on-coming breezes and other boats, and coach....in a carefully controlled, modular tone. Only I knew when he was frustrated.

When I was old enough to skip a more challenging form of inland lake scow, with crew members of my own choosing, my father scrutinized my every move from a respectable distance. But there was a painstaking debriefing on the home pier after every single race. Why had I changed tack suddenly in the middle of a relatively steady and promising breeze? If my answer sounded strategic, related to another boat or a guess about a wind change, I was o.k. Mistakes were for learning. The problem was... I often simply didn't know why I did what I did.

Dad and I were in perfect agreement about my basic condition. We both loved sailing. The feel of a slender, graceful scow with as much sail as could be handled safely, slicing through the waves, responding to the shifts and impulses of midwestern winds, brought immense joy to us both. We were one in the sheer pleasure of it. But for me, focusing on the breeze, the water, and the whole process of dancing with the wind, was enough. I had no will to compete with other sailors and other boats. My father knew this and respected it.

What I can see now with clarity is that there was/is a profound spiritual dimension to sailing, to what my father and I experienced together. He knew this but wisely let it happen without specific comment. In recent years, as I have finally awakened to the profound reality, movement and reciprocity of the Holy Spirit, I recognize that the winds of earth and water have a very similar mystery, rhythm, and pattern. Has it been easier for me to await, allow, accept and attend to the Motion of Love and its joys and sorrows because of those early sailing experiences ?

The answer is yes. Let me try to explain why by sharing the fundamental lessons I learned in my dance with the earth winds.

Number one: I have no control of the wind. As Jesus told Nicodemus, the earth winds blow where and as they will. They fluctuate, change, disappear. But, sooner or later, they return. They can be trusted.

So it is, Nicodemus learned too, with the winds of the Spirit. (John 3:8)

Number two: There is a moment, just prior to the emergence of a new wind, when the sailor, who trusts, intuits when, where and even how the new breeze will be. There are intimations, hints, an inner knowing which come from somewhere, something. It might be a touch of air against the cheek, a quality of smell or sound, a slight ruffling of the water beyond the boat. But in that brief time of inner and outward sensing, there is a guiding, a "still, small voice" which can be trusted.

So it is with the winds of the Spirit.

Number three: The guiding is an invitation to a dance. If we are able to respond, we will be blessed because we will be further taught and helped, and maybe, just maybe, we'll have a taste of co-creativity within the Motion of Love.

But response is not easy. First we must release all personal concerns, goals, expectations, illusions. Second, we must accept what comes including a timetable not of our own making or liking. Third, we must attend to what comes, stretching ourselves in any number of new ways, and never forgetting to give thanks.

In conclusion, in sharing my story of lessons about God learned in a sailboat, I am affirming that the natural world abounds in Loving Guidance. There are lessons in a garden, forest, alpine meadow, sunrise—particularly as the rhythm of life and death unfolds. Love surrounds and enfolds us all. Love is also within all of creation.

It is One Love, moving, guiding, dancing with us. Greet it in expectancy and joy. Joy will bless you in return.

The lessons of the Spirit from the Earth Winds are the four A's—Await, Allow, Accept and Attend, treasures from Julian of Norwich which came to me via writings from members of the Order of Julian.

Katharine Jacobsen *and her husband Ken were formerly directors of Pendle Hill. They currently are living in Delavan, Wisconsin, where they have a poustinia to which Midwestern Friends in need of spiritual direction frequently retreat.*

(*What Canst Thou Say?* November 2012
"Children's Mystical Experiences")

Silence Is The Holy Circle
Joyce Povolny

Why do we run from the silence,
The vast dome and the stars,
The absolute still,
Away, away, far from us?
Why are we glad at the sound
Of the lapping waters
And the wind
Whispering little nothings
In the tree tops?
Do we think that silence
Is the same as a void,
A void which when filled,
Could shake us
To our foundations?
We know in our souls
(The ultimate premonition, no doubt)
That silence is the sacred circle
In which God is the lone dancer,
Inviting each one of us—
Without exception—
To be his partner
And few of us, if any, have courage enough
To say, "I will, my Lord,"
And so stay His foot
From stepping out the holy circle.

Joyce Povolny has been a Quaker since 1958. She finds that Quakerism fits her soul and is the foundation from which her poetry comes to her.

(*What Canst Thou Say?* February 2004
"Touched by the Spirit")

Star Dust

Faith Paulsen

The night domes, a Bach Fugue. One of us
lifts her iPhone like the Statue of Liberty. She
has an app that identifies the stars. "That red one?
That's Venus," she says.
We pause, expand.
Someone says he read somewhere that
all the elements came into existence at the Big Bang:
carbon, oxygen, the whole periodic table,
ashes from furnaces where stars died.
The atoms of our own bodies—found poetry,
sculpted from smithereens. We point, draw circles on the
Jackson Pollock sky, and, like children
who take turns cupping a flashlight in their hands,
we marvel how skin glows red as Venus.
Our eyes contain Cezanne apples, our bloodcells novels,
ideas doing performance art all around our DNA,
and someone says, "Joni Mitchell was right,"
and Hamlet, and Leonardo, and Thich Nhat Hanh.
Our parted lips accept the stardust,
and it seems, tonight, we are **golden**.

Faith Paulsen is a writer and a member of Gwynedd Friends Meeting in Gwynedd, Pennsylvania. This poem was inspired by a magical evening with dear friends from that meeting, and was an honorable mention in the *Philadelphia Inquirer* Poetry Contest in April 2012.

(*What Canst Thou Say?* August 2012 "Unity")

The God of Wet Things

Glynis Lumb

I hadn't wanted to go to meeting that day. I had been feeling uneasy and vulnerable. I felt like I had been asking for an answer to my concern regarding our new clerk of meeting. It had been a quiet meeting.

I began to center down. It was an easy day, but I was aware of everyone in the room, like we were all one. I sat between Creedle and Mala in the second row. I felt a pulling and heaviness at my right side, toward Mala, who is often in pain and I thought I was feeling her message. So I sat with it and tried to lean into the feeling, to surround it and be it. Then I felt it let up and a heavy burden was on my head, pushing me down, like an elephant had sat down upon my head. I was very disturbed by it, but put love into it and tried to feel its weight with love. But, I was definitely overwhelmed and uncomfortable. Then, it let loose and I was light, very light, as if we were all light rather than heavy. And my eyes saw brightly, like the sun had come out.

Then the vision formed almost straight away. *It began with a cool, clear sparkling water. I was there in the water and viewing it at the same time. It was so clear, and sweet, and surrounded by warm rock. It was an endless pool of sparkling water. Then the vision grew in size as if I were no longer having the view of just one being, but of many, of every sentient being on Earth. My body was gone and I was lifted up with urgency and the words began to form to describe the vision and the emotion that was flowing through the body of the message.*

There is a term we use, "way will open." And this is how it is coming to me today. *There are aquifers deep down below the surface of the earth. They are cool, clear, sparkling, and pure. It takes hundreds of years to become this pure. The water filters down through rocks and dirt. It filters through grass, flowers, trees, and air, even through our bodies. It must filter through everything in order to be this clean. And it is gentle. It is patient.*

This is the meaning of "way will open." And it is gentle.

I sat down exhausted and not relieved of the message. I wept like my mother had died, for what seemed like a long time. My body could not find grounding. I couldn't sit in the chair. I stood up and walked around to the back of the room and lay down on the floor as flat as I could, my hands at my side like in yoga. I cried some more. I listened and took solace in the fifty some odd Friends holding the presence in the room. I waited for someone else to finish the message for me so I could be relieved. Finally, a woman stood up and shared a message about a cat. About how our Quaker meeting was like many cats going around doing whatever they wanted and assuming others should care as much for their actions. I laughed and was astonished by her truth. She seemed exasperated.

As meeting came to a close, I realized I couldn't get grounded because the vision I had was too big for me. It felt as if the message was too big for my small frame. Words were not able to describe what I had experienced. I sat with a friend in privacy for a bit after this and tried to use words to communicate what had happened. I was like someone who had been through a near death experience.

I had felt such beauty and truth manifested and yet it was so far from what felt like here and now. It felt like the earth was being raped and that it was my own mother. It was terrible. The answer was wrapped up in sorrow and urgency to speak the truth. The vision included *the gentle hand of God, of the energy that loves and enlivens all things. The gentle strength of water being a part of all things, ever flowing and telling us that we are all connected and what flows through one person flows through us all. The water must remain sacred and pure. It must be left alone deep under the rocks and clay. Clean water is essential to life.*

The only way for me to settle would be to continue to visualize this image of all that was wrong and all that was right. The beauty of all living things was being brutally attacked by the simple act of not waiting gently for a way forward. The violence of this was echoed in our very way of being with one another and with the Earth in the United States. There is violence in our search for fuel, minerals, oil, and coal. There is violence in the way we torture suspects for their secrets. There is violence in the way we raise our children with disrespect. There is violence in the upsurge of C-sections in America. There is violence in the way we judge others, rather than wait for deeper understanding. And we can all feel this violence in our very being, because we are made of water. The water knows how it is being treated.

It was a message of hope. It was a message for me to carry for myself as well. It would lay in wait for a time when this sense would bring a witness to truth. It gave me certainty that non-violence is a vital way to move through this world as human beings. That the only way to be whole, healthy, and filled with light is to consider all of us, connected, heard, in every decision we make to move forward. We are capable of a glorious beauty out of all of this brutality.

Glynis (Glee) Lumb is an artist and a member of Multnomah Meeting, Portland, Oregon. She blogs at <gleebeans-gleebeans.blogspot.com>.

(*What Canst Thou Say?* May 2013 "Meaning from Despair")

A Friend of the Darkness
Christine O'Brien

The moon is a friend of the darkness. Some creatures come alive and live their entire lives in darkness. Fireflies and stars would not astound us without darkness. As for me I have pulled my chair up to the door opening onto the garden and watched long into the night as the twilight and then the night descend over all. At some point the trees become silhouettes in the darkening sky and the colors fade. Darkness smoothes over all of the imperfections and makes a magic world of shadows and darker shadows.

I can walk through my house in darkness and lay my hand on what I want. I take a strange pride in that. Darkness is beautiful to me and often I am called outside to walk with my arms reaching overhead as though I could touch the sky, tickling the stars with my fingertips. Other times I hold my arms wide open in simple love and gratitude.

However, when I am very ill with little chance of being well, soon the darkness can seem very long indeed. Sometimes I feel that this night could be my last and I consider the mystery of change that touches all. Death and thoughts of death are also friends of the darkness. I have not made perfect peace with my death or the death of others, but I do not want to "rage against the dying of the light." I want to "go gently into that good night." I want to make friends with this mystery and let it work some grace in me that will turn me always towards gratitude.

And what of the darkness in the hearts and lives of those who bring me their sorrows and fears? What of the darkness in our world that seems to grow larger the more we know about it? I hope to be guided in what I am called to do. Though I believe we can "listen each other into wholeness," I have never seen my light eliminate the depth of darkness that has shaped someone's soul. I hope that in walking the path a ways together and holding each other up with a tender hand we will find resting places and friends along the way.

I believe each of us can be cradled "in the everlasting arms" that seem more present in the darkness. The earth turns to darkness every day dressing our lives in dark velvet. Soft darkness whispers over me and is my rest. I too am a friend of the darkness.

If I say "let only darkness cover me, and light around me be night," even darkness is not dark to thee; the night is as bright as the day, for darkness is as light with thee. (Psalms 139:11-12)

Christine O'Brien *is working on creating Circus McGurkis the People's Fair, which is thirty-three years old and is sponsored by St. Petersburg Meeting.*

(*What Canst Thou Say?* November 2004 "Darkness")

A Committed Life

> Here I am. Lord. Is it I, Lord?
> I have heard you calling in the night.
> I will go, Lord, if you lead me.
> I will hold your people in my heart.
> (*Worship in Song: A Friends Hymnal,*
> Friends General Conference, 1996, p. 260)

Meet some deeply committed lovers of God, who have taken mystic vows of marriage. Our authors all give their God-given gifts back to God, and to the world. It is love that inspires our authors to commit their lives, in spite of fears both known and unknown.

Mike Resman describes his retirement to a full-time career of praying. Zarinea Lee Zolivea, faced with an unpleasant work environment, slowly sees her prayers for harmony and compatibility come to fruition. Elizabeth K. Gordon chooses to accompany a teen mother of triplets into an uncertain future. Elizabeth De Sa is called to gardening; Erin McDougall is called to see God manifested in everything; and Judy Lumb integrates her spiritual with her scientific side.

Robin Harper cares for abandoned animals while Kathleen Maia Tapp hears the prayer of our endangered earth; Phil Fitz is called to live so that God is obvious in the world through him; and Peg Morton is called by God to fast for disabled people on the steps of the capitol building. James Baker comes to understand that his hands are his gifts from God, and through giving them to God, he lives for God. Maurine Pyle commits her life to God knowing only that she will be led, but not where. Rhonda Pfaltzgraff-Carlson is calling us to know God inwardly, so that Life can become manifest in our social structures.

These authors have heard God calling in the night, and ask only that God lead them.

A Full-time Career

Michael Resman

Some years ago I retired to pursue a new career—praying. This might seem somewhat abstract and of questionable utility, given that I was stepping away from serving children with disabilities. Yet, for those who believe in the power of prayer, there's benefit in engaging in it full time.

Prayer for me began quite simply. I was invited to adopt a spiritual discipline as part of a spiritual nurture program. I chose daily prayer, and for a year didn't put much effort into it. Some days, I forgot. Others, I spent only a few minutes saying "Hi" to God or rushing through a list of requests.

Reporting back to others in my group month after month that I was a slacker pushed me to become more deliberate. Prayer times expanded to twenty, then forty-five minutes, and I found myself at peace, resting in God's arms. I'd start by praying for a list of people, then sought simply to be with the One.

When it came time to retire, I re-read Brother Lawrence, wishing I could pray continually. I focused on Brother Lawrence's efforts to continually think about and talk with God. I quickly discovered that I lack the discipline to keep turning my mind to God.

Instead I prayed more informally, seeking God in my surroundings as I went about my daily activities. I continued the practice of beginning prayer sessions asking for God's mercy for a list of people. This pulled me into a deep silence, sometimes for several hours.

Prayer walks in a local park helped me reach through the veil between this world and the next. Cross stitching while listening to sacred choral music brought peace and joy.

After six months I discovered that I was praying continually, but not with my mind. My heart was constantly turned to my Beloved.

Brother Lawrence had said, "…I regarded God as the goal and end of all the thoughts and affections of my soul."

I had focused on believing I had to think about and talk with God all the time and became discouraged when I couldn't. What I could do was love God, always. How encouraging, that there is this sweet path of heart-prayers that can lead to living continually in God's presence.

Billions of people pray to the Divine in a myriad of ways. For me, the most important aspect of prayer is its intention. When we pray to overcome illness—or the opposing football team—we remain rooted on this earth. When we seek to connect with God, to love God, we can be transported.

Perhaps you're thinking that this sounds quite self-absorbed, and wonder what good prayer efforts do for the world. I have "seen" a spiritual wind blowing through me, as it blows through each of us. As it does we alter it for good or ill and affect our surroundings. Am I adding peace, harmony, compassion and forgiveness to the world, or their opposites?

When I'm praying—clinging to the One—I'm content in being a vessel for good, whether or not my efforts are visible or even understandable to others.

Michael Resman *is an editor of WCTS, and author of Pendle Hill pamphlet # 390,* Special Education as a Spiritual Journey.

(*What Canst Thou Say?* February 2011 "Prayer")

Visualizing Harmony and Compatibility

Zarinea Lee Zolivea

Not too long ago, I was almost unable to work because I experienced two new co-workers as unusually negative and downright mean. Their conversations centered on putting down other teachers and many of the children at the school.

I did not want to complain to my supervisor. In my mind, it seemed that if I just kept on praying, circumstances would improve, but they kept getting worse.

A dear friend of mine had recommended *The Thought Bricks Course*. As things were getting difficult with my colleagues I received another lesson via mail. The new lesson told of a spiritual exercise that would transform difficult working conditions. Basically, the practice required that you visualize yourself facing the difficult person in a vertical tunnel with a white light beaming from the top to the bottom. Holding this vision, you stayed centered until you felt great peace and joy. The end result was a smile of gratitude.

Joyfully, I did the suggested exercise morning and evening. I visualized compatibility and harmony between myself and the difficult teachers. I pictured myself and them smiling and happy. It was not enough to pray and visualize. It was recommended that actually feeling the results was very important. I practiced in my mind what I wished to happen between myself and the two teachers. I "saw" all of us happy and talking amicably with each other. Knowing that there is no time in Divine mind, I waited with positive expectancy. This is also part of the practice.

Then one day, I noticed a slight change for the better on the part of the two troublesome teachers. Both of them were actually smiling. They began to be more pleasant in their conversation with me. There was less criticism of the children and the staff from them. I felt relief and joy to view the outpouring of a spiritual practice in action.

As the days moved forward, my working conditions were transformed as my attitude changed from a negative state of mind to a positive one. The joy I once had when just thinking about going to work returned to me with greater anticipation than I had experienced before.

A prayer of thanks will always go out to the course I took, the spiritual practices, and most of all, the belief that difficulties can be transformed through faith and practice.

Zarinea Lee Zolivea is an attender at Claremont (CA) Friends Meeting. She is a retired educator and writes poetry, short articles, and children's stories. To find out more about the The Thought Bricks Course, contact Bernard, Thought Bricks Teaching Centre, Altarnun, Launceston, Cornwall, England.

(*What Canst Thou Say?* February 2007
"Spirituality in the Workplace")

Walk with Her

Elizabeth K. Gordon

I should have prayed, meditated, walked for as long and as far as it took for fear to turn loose my heart. I didn't. I went up to my third floor room and wrote this in my journal: "I don't feel entirely clear to go ahead with having the babies come home here. My motives are definitely unclear. A friend warned that while I might think I could handle it, I probably can't. She dreamt me walking away from it all and warned that I might do that. She's probably right. It's hard though to let go of the idea." I still have that file. It's dated February 8th, eight days before the triplets were born....

The next day Kaki took Lamarr to lunch and told him that we still wanted to help, but we had changed our minds about Tahija coming home to our house with the boys. I called Tahija's grandmother Agnes Grealy and told her the same thing. She said we'd done more than most would have; we should feel okay.

I didn't feel okay. I dreaded facing Tahija. I found her propped on pillows between the stacked monitors and a pushed-aside food tray, eyes closed, a palm on her forehead. A grayness had come to her face, like a film of dust on mahogany. I thought of the girl I'd seen walking toward me across the parking lot that first day, Tweetie Bird in her arms, a bounce in her step. She looked so much more than three months older.

"Hey," she said when she saw me, opening her eyes briefly. "You want this pudding?"

I looked into the cup. "Nasty." ...I told her how much we liked her, how interested we were in her life and well-being, how willing we were to continue helping.

"You're putting me out," she said.

"We can help with first and last, security deposit, all that, and if you need babysitters— "

"They're not going to let me live on my own, Kath-a-ryn."

"Who 'they'?"

"DHS!" She spoke in a stream: "If I don't have verifiable income—verifiable income, not help—they going to declare me unfit, an unfit parent. I told you minors can't get welfare now unless they living with an adult, so how I'm going to show verifiable income if I'm not getting a check and then I'm an unfit parent, see? They'll be waiting in the delivery room, take them right out the doctor's hands."

She looked me in the eye until I saw—the underside of the hawk, the splayed talons, the greedy beak....I left....

Late that night, on the third floor of the row house we had shared before she went into the hospital, I turned off the light and pulled my chair up to the window. In the park, lamplight lay like frost on the branches of the bare trees. From a telephone wire near the window a pair of white leather sneakers hung by their laces, the lower one turning slowly, the upper still, as if poised mid-step. A pigeon perched on the wire and began to groom itself, setting the sneakers swaying. They lulled me like a hypnotist's pendulum, and I found myself remembering a Quaker meeting in New Paltz, New York. Twenty or so silent people on plain wooden benches facing the unornamented center of a plain room. The silence ran unbroken for a time, and then deepened suddenly, as a stream opening into a deep pool.

Sitting within this silence, I had seemed to drift into a sort of movie, more conceptual than visual, but I felt I could see the concepts, in a way. They were outlined against a patina of sadness, a sadness that seemed to be around me but not in me, at first. What I saw was American history as a series of missed opportunities to right the wrong of slavery ...

A Committed Life ◄ 43

- ... *Noble ideals yet glowing red and gold from the forge of revolution, bent so soon with hypocrisy.*
- ... *Indentured servitude, by self-serving law changed to slavery (for the African servants only), and that becoming uniquely North American chattel slavery.*
- ... *Not following even slow England's lead and ending slavery, but importing more and more people, breeding them like animals.*
- ... *The Abolitionists, yes, and service on the Underground Railroad, but the back bench too.*
- ... *Proclaim LIBERTY throughout all the Land unto all the Inhabitants thereof.*
- ... *The Civil War, a nation wrenched apart, and when freedom was bought at such a ghastly price to let it slip away.*
- ... *Reconstruction, not the caricature but an amazing oasis, democracy proven, tried and proven and betrayed, into the hands of the insurrectionists.*
  If Lincoln hadn't been killed...
  if forty acres and a mule had been given...
- ... *if slave pensions had become a reality...*
- ... *if land grants had been granted to the freedmen too, as Sojourner Truth dreamed...*
- ... *if Jim Crow terror hadn't been allowed to run on so long...*
- ... *generations with no vote, no schools, hunger, flight ...*
- ... *if the cities fled to had opened their arms or given at least the grudging welcome the cheap-labor immigrants were given...*
- ... *if the labor unions hadn't slammed their doors...*
- ... *if the nation had respected the black vets coming home from Europe...*
- ... *had given pensions and home loans and farm loans fairly...*
- ... *if the schools had been desegregated when the court of the land decreed them desegregated...*
- ... *381 days walking to get a seat on the bus... thirty-nine years old!*
- ... *Hoover blocking death threats,*
- ... *police cars circling a hotel in Memphis...*
- ... *Marian Anderson on the steps of the Lincoln Memorial, "Sweet Land of Liberty,"*
- ... *if only King ...*
- ... *if only Malcolm...*
- ... *Rodney King on every television,*

... and so many prime-time times a night men of color in cuffs,
... men and teenagers with their faces to the sidewalk,
... the chain as through shackled ankles running back through every era of America's making.

Quaking, I rose to speak about what I'd seen in the silence. Only a fragment, it was enough; when I sat the quaking stopped and my breath was given back to me.

Sitting, eyes closed, I had prayed then as one washed ashore. Let me do something, let no new harm be done, let the wounds be healed, let us not miss the next opportunity, let me not miss my opportunity. Use me. Change me. Use me. If the Underground Railroad was shut down too soon . . . if this nation, conceived in liberty (what love I felt then for my country!) and dedicated, dedicated to the proposition . . . . In the silence that day, sitting on the hard bench beside a white woman who'd moved her small children into Mississippi's Freedom Summer and a man who tried to live the Sermon on the Mount, I was blessed with a clear perception, and responded with a clear prayer . . . to which Tahija coming into my life seemed an answer.

Miss not your opportunity.

In Philadelphia, I opened my eyes. The pigeon was gone. The sneakers were turning like a wind vane in the wind. *Walk with her*, I heard (a gentle voice). *Walk with her.*

But would she ever want to walk with me again? I didn't know. Kaki was at a meeting. I didn't wait for her to come home. I knew she'd be glad I had changed my mind, and it seemed to me Tahija was the first person I should tell. So I threw on boots, coat and hat and headed for the El. I wanted to knock at every door and announce it: They've been born, the triplets have been born, they're fine, they're coming home, here.

Unless I've blown it.

Had I blown it? I felt like Scrooge after his three-ghost night. If I got another chance, I sure wasn't going to blow it again.

Elizabeth K. Gordon *was on the editorial team of* WCTS *until the triplets were born. (Excerpted from* Walk With Us: Triplet Boys, Their Teen Parents, and Two White Women Who Tagged Along.*)*

(*What Canst Thou Say?* August 2007 "Hospitality")

On Being Called

Elizabeth De Sa

A few years ago I was praying under a tree. Although young, it had an aged wisdom beyond my years. It was a time of inner turmoil for me, and I sought the consolation of this tree often. I watched bulbous green fruits growing on its slender branches, until one day one dropped in front of me. I had no doubt—the fruit was a gift. Slowly I picked it up, smelled it and ran my tongue over the silky, minutely hairy skin. A thin white milk exuded from its crown. My eyes caressed its gentle curves. I had no idea if it was edible but I decided to trust the spirit in which it was given. I peeled it slowly, savoring its silent grip loosening as skin separated from fruity flesh. I ate what was proffered, black-maroon flesh riddled with fine white seeds, luxuriously, juice tantalizing my lips. Its sweetness, its deep earthy flavor fed the bubbling energy at my core, the rising of which thrills me as it surges through my body—I feel most alive when I am connected with the Divine in all.

It was my first mindful eating experience, a glimpse into a constant state of divine being. I wasn't thinking about being mindful; it happened naturally when I was in a state of divine listening. The fig was a gift of love from sun, earth, and tree. It fed my body and soul.

A few months later, I left my life in Australia for a year of spiritual exploration at Pendle Hill. The two years prior had been filled with angst about not fitting into society, and seeking deep spiritual satiation for a hunger that was consuming every moment.

There is much joy in following a calling. I also felt relief to be free from earth-quaking depressions as my soul called for outer alignment with its innermost workings. But I did not grow complacent. Having experienced the Divine in nature, my soul yearned for divine communion in all—I aspired to be guided, to follow paths that led me to deeper connectedness. But it takes time to understand the human condition, the divine mission, my gifts and callings. They were revealed as I was ready.

At Pendle Hill, I explored contemplative prayer, meditation, mysticism, arts, Quaker testimonies and activism. I then took a position teaching Environmental Science at a Quaker high school semester program on peace, social justice and environmental sustainability. I passionately developed a curriculum exploring the science of the environment, environmental use, abuse, anthropocentrism, and spiritual ecology. I was passionate about the material and I cared a great deal about the earth, my students and how to live joyously and sustainably on this planet. Yet that was not enough.

The depression did not return but the angst did. I grew negative in my perceptions and I felt cheated. I was assigning papers that I wanted to write; I was tired and did not have enough energy or time to connect with the Divine, and I was tired of talking about sustainability—I wanted to practice it. Through meditation, I saw that my perception was clouded by callings that were not being followed. Having been gifted with divine experiences, I seek to reside constantly in that place of deep connectedness. My deepest wish for life is to attain inner peace.

Similar to my decision to go to Pendle Hill, I again decided to turn contemplative: not just for a year, but as an answer to my soul's calling, as a way of life. Since I was 5 years old, I have wanted to be a writer. I feel alive when I am writing, it is the medium through which I perceive and inspire. Yet it is a gift I have often ignored; for too long I have only valued things I find challenging or cannot do, and tried to push myself into teaching jobs that "stretch myself." This time I decided to accept myself instead. I cut my hours, took a salary cut—from $20,000 to $2,000 per year—and became the gardening intern. By following inward callings rather than outward expectations, characteristics that had been limitations became gifts—I allowed myself to soar and my Light to shine.

I am infinitely happy in my new role. I begin at sunrise with meditation, then a long writing session before moving out to the garden. As I water the plants, I become aware of the water I drink filling me with the prayer I pour into it. As I gather and eat fresh kale, I am filled with awe and gratitude. I have a relationship with plants through all their life stages. I am a nurturer and facilitator of their growth; they are equally so in mine, a symbiotic relationship of love and need. At university I studied Biology objectively. Yet here in my garden, as I build my compost, and feel its heat surrounding me as I turn it, I feel a part of life, death and rebirth. Eating is now an inherently mindful practice.

I'm experiencing a newfound parallel between my working life and my spiritual life. The land teaches me the harmonious and natural principles of co-operation. I aspire to speak the language of enough rather than excessive desire. There is a synchronicity here with my need for simplicity, of connecting with the Divine in nature, and learning from the wisdom of the wilderness. The spirit that is alive and heaving in all of creation surrounds me. I listen and learn through intuition. I play with plant spirits and they guide me in nurturing a beautiful garden beyond my knowledge and experience.

In this time of food insecurity—when agribusinesses destroy more than they grow, when petroleum-based farming paves the way to war, when corporations control seeds and plant genomes, gardening is a political and spiritual move. And writing is my prayer of authenticity.

I am blessed with learning, time, quiet to hear God's voice, solitude, community, abundant life energy, stimuli for inspiration and growth, and unfolding inner peace.

Elizabeth De Sa *is a Young Adult Friend of Indian descent raised in the UK. She attends Grass Valley Meeting in California. Her daily spiritual practices are meditation, contemplative prayer and writing.*

(*What Canst Thou Say?* February 2008 "Called")

Called on the Day of My Conception
Erin McDougall

I was called into the world by God on the day of my conception. Like every child, I was born with a Divine spark shining within me, not yet honed nor dampened by worldly learning and experience.

A little more than twelve years later, I began to define this presence that I had previously left unacknowledged. After some discernment with my dear grandmother, I identified myself as a part of my religious heritage and determined that I was, like my mother before me, a Friend.

It wasn't until two weeks after my thirteenth birthday that I heard the call again. It was more audible this time and required my complete attention. Something deep in my body, a place of knowing beyond any place I had been aware of before that moment, spoke softly to me as my world turned upside down. As doctors told me that I had cancer, God assured me that this was part of my journey. This was the beginning of my work.

My belief is that the "seal of Divinity" (as William Penn called it) is placed on us the moment we come into being. We are born into the world understanding the sanctity of our Self deep within our souls, embedded in our muscular tissue and skeletal structure. Unfortunately, almost immediately we begin the process of forgetting.

We spend the rest of our lives relearning what it means to be a child of God and a member of this earth-family. The process of hearing and responding to our calling in life is part of this re-learning. As we begin to re-learn who we are as people, especially in relationship to others, our ability to be present to our relationship with God grows.

In a perfect world, this is the moment in time when we would all claim our true selves, step into our own skin with joy and confidence, and embody the original calling that we heard when we came into being in this world.

Intimacy with God

This is not a perfect world.

For years after finishing my chemotherapy treatments, I was completely lost. The devil, in this case, had many forms, but ultimately was anything that would take me further off the road that I glimpsed briefly when I was first diagnosed.

As I journeyed back from that dark place, I began to find pieces of my true self again. The first traceable step in the reclaiming of my life's purpose came when I left behind everything I knew to delve into five months at Pendle Hill. The call to go to Pendle Hill came in the night, jolted me out of a deep sleep and had me repeating the call into the empty air around me. It was not a question of having heard God right, nor a question if I should follow. So, hardly knowing where Philadelphia was on a map, and having never lived outside of Canada, I got on a plane less than a month later to begin this new chapter of my life.

The call to Earlham School of Religion came in a similarly startling form, leaving me shaking and weeping in the middle of a class during my time at Pendle Hill. I found many excuses for why this was not going to happen but when each dilemma that might keep me from this work was miraculously solved, I could no longer avoid God's nudging.

I have been offered many opportunities to work through the fear to live into God's will. One such opportunity came with a leading to travel in the ministry last summer together with Friend Andrew Essex-Haines.

As is true of any travel in the ministry, we quickly found that the reasons that we thought we were at gatherings were not, in fact, the reasons that God had brought us to that place. God used us in numerous ways, some of which we are slowly identifying and some that we will never know.

Perhaps the greatest thing I have been blessed with is the deep knowledge that God is in everything. God has been in every moment of my life, not just present when I am shaken to the bone by the magnitude of what I am called to do.

I was called into this world by God on the day of my conception, as we all are. Each step of my journey is a small piece of a much larger calling: to see God manifested in everything and to fully live into the Self I was meant to be. Everything else is merely details.

Erin McDougall *was born and raised in Vancouver, Canada. She is currently a student at Earlham School of Religion, completing a Masters of Divinity with an emphasis in Pastoral Care and Counseling. One of the things that brings her joy is to create glass art using broken windows and other media.*

(*What Canst Thou Say?* February 2008 "Called")

Collecting Parts of Myself
Judy Lumb

I am a mystic and a scientist, a practical person with a strong spiritual need, a biomedical laboratory scientist with a calling to save the earth, a cancer researcher with an aversion to our economic system based upon infinite growth. Even as a 12-year-old in confirmation class, I knew that there were two disparate parts of myself and assumed that "never the twain shall meet." I was drawn to the Sermon on the Mount and found "Love your Enemy" to be a challenging motto that I hoped would be the basis of my life. Then they wanted me to say these words, "I believe ...", but I resisted, wondering, "Is there a God? Was Jesus divine? Did all that really happen? How can I say I believe it?"

The first hint of resolution to this dichotomy was an asymptote in analytical geometry. A curved line approaching a straight line, always halving the distance, will never reach the line. I could prove mathematically the existence of infinity and it was not a difficult jump to the assertion, "God is infinity," and then "God is love."

But what about Jesus? An approach to this issue came from a series of sermon poems on Genesis given by B. Davie Napier, who was the Chaplain at Stanford University. These beautiful poems were published in the book, *Come, Sweet Death* (1966). Napier said that a myth describes things that "never were, but always are." Treating the Bible as myth gave me a way to approach the Jesus questions.

The mystical part of myself was reawakened by my friend and scientific colleague Judy Bender when we began meditating during lunch breaks at various places around the university. This coincided with my commitment to regular attendance at Atlanta Friends Meeting, so contemplation became a major part of my life.

I finally pulled together my mystical side with my scientific side when I read the Preface to *Friends for Three Hundred Years: The History and Beliefs of the Society of Friends Since George Fox Started the Quaker Movement*, by Howard Brinton (1952). Brinton explains that the distinction between mystics and other religious persons is that mystics believe in their own experiences while other established religions require beliefs as determined by some human authority. He goes on to say that is the same as scientists who believe in the results of their experiments, rather than some established authority. Bringing these two together is the quotation where George Fox wrote, "I know this experimentally." Some people say that he really meant "experientially," but the original wording was a validation for me.

My overambitious desire to discover a cure for cancer came before I finished high school, but as I went through the academic training as a scientist I became discouraged because it was only possible to do a proper experiment on a tiny piece of the larger puzzle at any one time. The variables were endless. How would we ever solve the cancer puzzle? My husband was working on computer models of water resources, which gave me the idea to apply that methodology to my cancer research. I began to call myself an "integrationist," always trying to pull things together. Since I was a European-American teaching in an African-American university, that concept had a racial component, too.

My calling as an environmentalist came a little later, just in time for the first Earth Day in 1970, but it wasn't too far afield from cancer research, as cancer is one result of our misuse of Earth. I did wonder why I chose a field of study that kept me locked inside a laboratory all day instead of outside in nature. But weekends, vacations, and exposure to deep ecology gave me the experience of unity of all things on Earth. That experience has led me to work for co-management of protected areas by indigenous people, preservation of indigenous cultures, and reform of our economic system which is based upon infinite growth on a finite planet.

Reading the Pendle Hill pamphlet *John Yungblut: Passing the Mystical Torch* by Charlie Finn, reminded me of another great contribution to the collection of parts of myself. John Yungblut was the Program Director of Atlanta Friends Meeting in the late 1950s and early 1960s, the Civil Rights days. He returned to Atlanta to give a workshop in the early 1980s on his concepts of evolutionary Christianity. This was another watershed moment for me as he used the concept of a myth as something that is not fixed, but can continue to evolve. He distinguishes the fixed historical Jesus from the myth of the inward Christ, drawing on the mysticism of Rufus Jones, evolutionary approach of Pierre Teilhard de Chardin, and depth psychology of Carl Jung. In his last Pendle Hill pamphlet, *For That Solitary Individual: An Octogenarian's Counsel on Living and Dying*, Yungblut shows how using the mythical approach allows for human evolution, which gives us great hope for the future.

"The contemporary world scene may certainly foster pessimism, but in the context of evolution, there is ground for optimism. ... There is an inescapable connection between contemplative prayer and motivation to engage in social reform. It is contemplative prayer that confirms the inseparable unity of all things."

Judy Lumb *is still a member of Atlanta Friends Meeting, although she has lived in Belize since 1987. She serves on the* What Canst Thou Say *editorial team.*

(*What Canst Thou Say?* August 2012 "Unity")

It's Just An Animal

Robin W. Harper

Many people have a soft spot in their heart for animals, and I am one of them. As a child, going to zoos was a mixed experience—enjoyment at seeing the animals, sadness at their confinement. I felt like they looked at me and let me feel their predicament—as if to say, "You know this isn't right!" It made me feel like I had a special responsibility to them. Also, seeing a dead animal on the side of the road was particularly painful. A deer, legs sprawled in an unnatural position, head or rump crushed on the pavement, made my chest tighten.

I have always felt a bit of shame and guilt for noticing the suffering of animals above that of people, and for feeling that animals are somehow more to me than humans are. I remember being gently made fun of for it: "Robin is so tender-hearted," "Those big eyes get her every time," "What would you do, let them all run loose?" etc.

I began to feel differently about my sensitivity on the night I saw a litter of almost-grown kittens hiding in the grass of a drive-through at a fast food restaurant. I desperately wished I had something to feed them. So I did what felt like a really crazy thing—I went to the nearby grocery, bought some cat food, and went back and fed them. I was very much afraid that someone was going to be angry with me, for trespassing and also perhaps for possibly attracting rodents, although you'd know there was no fear of this if you had seen how they scarfed that food up! Despite my fears, I decided to let myself go ahead and buy dog and cat food to keep in my car, in case I was ever in that situation again.

I began to stop and feed stray animals whenever I saw them, always feeling guilty and a little bit scared. As I coaxed the dog or cat (mostly dogs) to come closer and trust me, I would argue in my head with anyone who might come along and take issue with me. My intuition was pretty clear that I was right, but I was constantly mentally justifying my actions. Some of these arguments went like this:

"This dog cannot go home with me. I already have four of my own. I will not take it to the shelter, because that means death."

"This dog has no collar, so there's no returning it to its owner. You can see it has no desire to be 'rescued'—he's staying at a safe distance, waiting for me to leave the food and go."

"This dog is suffering! Look how skinny! He is not going to leave anything behind to attract rodents."

"This is not 'just a dog.' He can feel pain and fear and hunger just like you and me. None of God's creatures deserve to suffer like this, no matter how insignificant."

Gradually over the months and years of doing this, I began to realize that this was not just something I wanted to do, but something I had to do. Whenever I tried to convince myself I couldn't stop to help an animal because I was running late or there were people who would see me, it was no good. Invariably I would have to turn around and go back. One day I finally realized that this was my ministry. I wish I could remember the words God said to me on that day. It was something along the lines of "Just do it." I do remember hearing, "Who else is going to do this, if not you?" The feeling of shame was lifted from me. I felt I could at last name what I was doing. It felt pretty obvious then, that that was why I was always compelled to notice them, that that was why I had the "looking at me" experience—I was supposed to do something about it!

I was reminded of the verse from Matthew, "Whatsoever ye do unto the least of these my brethren, ye do unto me." I also thought of the message of St. Theresa, to do small things with great love. At last I knew I was doing God's work, even in this tiny way.

Of course, the job quickly grew beyond just feeding. Now it's also trying to find owners, if the dog is lost. It's picking them up and fostering them, if they clearly want more than a meal. It's getting them vet care, when they'll let me. Even though I make donations to the county animal shelter and the Humane Society every year, I try not to take them there if I can help it, because they are forced to euthanize so many animals. I have been blessed with great assistance from Independent Animal Rescue, the Coalition to Unchain Dogs, my vet, several no-kill shelters in the area, and many, many friends and family.

Others are called to be in the Peace Corps, to be doctors or social workers or teachers, to adopt children, to give to the many worthy humanitarian causes that are out there. But this is the job that God has given to me. I feel like crying with joy, just being able to write those words with confidence and faith!

Robin W. Harper *has been a member of Chapel Hill Friends Meeting since 2001. She says, "I could not do this work without the support of my wonderful husband. He's the reason I have boots in my car, in addition to dog and cat food—in case I need to follow dogs into the bush!" She tries (and often fails) to make time for silence every day.*

(*What Canst Thou Say?* May 2011 "Animals")

Prayer of the World

Kathleen Maia Tapp

I've written all my life—first children's novels, then a shift to poetry and essays. During a time when my spiritual life was opening, deepening and filled with energy, my dreams sent gentle messages that there would be another shift—and it would be about "writing the earth." I wasn't sure what that meant. I felt strong nudges to let my writing deepen. I went on retreat. There were many frustrations. I couldn't seem to open. I asked to stay another day. At the end of that day, I sat watching the sunset and trying to write, and then there was a shift, and it began to feel as if the sunset was writing me.

It was the voice of earth, stone, sea, wind, and the Mother of all speaking through creation, speaking of the web of life and the great strain on it, speaking of the deep and desperate need for prayer—an expanded meaning of prayer: "listening softens the fortress that guards the heart. When the heart softens, that is prayer. … the web of life is strengthened hand by hand, heart by heart, prayer by prayer." She also spoke through the colors of the rainbow; each color holding its own meaning. "The White Light of Love bends through the prism of itself and pours down color."

I felt overwhelmed by this writing. I participated in a women's pilgrimage to the sites of the Mother in Mexico, to learn more and to ask for help. Although I wanted to move ahead with sharing the writing, I felt fear and inner resistance. With support from mentoring Friends, I applied to the Way of Ministry program. The affirmation and support in this Spirit-filled program helped me shed my fear. I was surprised to find it replaced with…joy…

While I'd been writing, my husband Ken, had been deeply involved in his own spiritual practice, which was/is nature photography. We paired his luminous photographs with the Prayer of the World poetry, creating a presentation where his photographs moved across the screen while I read the poetry. And we discovered, as one Friend said, "Pairing the two media made each more transparent to that which is behind both of them." We found we had both opened to the same message.

Ken and Katharine Jacobsen, also involved in Way of Ministry program, have provided holy accompaniment and practical help in moving forward with this presentation, as have peer groups and care committees. Ken Jacobsen "listened" for a song of "Prayer of the World" and composed a beautiful, spirit-filled song. Peggy O'Neill, who teaches and leads sacred dance, is now "listening" for how this can be danced. Many are helping to raise this prayer of the world.

My husband and I continue on our "Earth World Pilgrimage." Over the past few years we've traveled to many places, including the Grand Canyon, the Everglades, and the Medicine Wheel in Wyoming. We've gone to the Smoky Mountains, the Great Lakes, the Mississippi River, and Pendle Hill. We just returned from the tundra in northern Canada. I have traveled to Ireland and Iona. At each place there is a "teaching."

I like the thought that perhaps earth is holding a Meeting for Worship; the messages coming from different sites all contribute to the whole message—how to open the heart, heal the web, join the prayer of life, help earth move into a new day, a new dawn. It is a message, ultimately, of love and hope:

...I lay you in the manger of a New Day
and I will guard your growth with love,
and I will give you the song
  of the stars, seas and stones,
    the tales of the winds
    to guide your growing days.

Kathleen Maia Tapp *is a pilgrim-poet and a former editor of WCTS.*

(*What Canst Thou Say?* February 2010 "A Covenant with Creation")

To Live God

Phil Fitz

God has always been important to me. I have had deep and direct experiences of God in meeting for worship. I have gone to God for support and guidance at key times in my life. But my relationship with God changed after my partner, Dan, died. My grieving was deep and hard, and I was unable to feel God through the pain. I felt like I was in an unrecognizable place, alone and bereft, sure that I had been abandoned by God. As the pain eased over time, I came to understand that God had been there all the time, holding me, giving me the strength and grace to go on. I realized that I had been closer to God during that time than at any time in my life, just unable to see God because I was so closely held that I could not see or recognize Him. I came to understand that I am a mere extension of God, and that it is in God that I live and move and have my being.

I began spending more time in prayer, as the only appropriate response of gratitude for God's goodness to me. I sought out times of retreat, to spend time alone with God. I went to a Trappist monastery for a weekend, where I felt joined deeply to these men who devoted their lives to prayer for no other reason than to love God. I understood what Thomas Merton meant when he talked about monasteries as the places that keep the world from coming apart.

After some months, my first instruction came: the word anchor kept rising. It was not clear to me what that meant. Am I to seek to anchor myself to God? Am I to anchor others to God? What forms might my call to anchor take? I was having lunch at a Shalem contemplative prayer program with people I had known for only a few days. The conversation was the sort of polite conversation one has with people one does not know well. For no clear reason, I changed the subject and began talking about reading Julian of Norwich, a 14th century anchoress who spent her life in solitude in prayer for a particular church. I talked about my call to be an anchor in some way. They were smiling and glancing at each other, and then told me they were lay members of the Order of Julian of Norwich, an Episcopal monastic contemplative order.

For some time, I considered joining a monastery. My call is like that of contemplative monastics—to spend my life with the central focus of loving God. But the form of the Catholic and Episcopal contemplative monasteries is not right for me. At my core I am Quaker, not Catholic or Episcopalian. I am to seek to live out that same call in a Quaker form. I was not meant to experience my call in the monasteries, but to follow my own path.

I knew my job was getting in the way of that call, and I kept waiting for a way to open. After much work in discerning my call, I realized that I had to step out without knowing the path, and that the time to do so had come. I have quit my job to spend the next few years full time in relationship with God. A clearness committee worked with me to discern a second instruction. With their help, I have discerned my purpose is to "live into an awareness of the presence of God."

Living out this instruction has led me into a different life. I move at a slower pace. I take hours in the morning to be in different forms of prayer: journaling, sitting, writing prayers, walking. Over time, my awareness of the presence of God has increased. Sometimes it is as though God is sitting beside me. Other times, I sense God rising up through me, filling me, like I am a glove on the hand of God. I am more aware of God in other people I meet passing on the sidewalk, working at the grocery store, walking a dog. I find that I can hold that awareness through simple physical day-to-day activities—washing dishes, raking leaves, cleaning the house, cooking, paying bills. I cannot seem to hold that awareness when I am too engaged in "my head," as in doing academic work for a biology paper I am writing. Perhaps I will grow into being able to hold onto my awareness of the presence of God when I am intellectually engaged, but I cannot now.

Recently I was given a third instruction. From a deep place, I was writing about a dream and what it might mean for the community. I easily recognized most of the 50 or so lines of the poem as being from me and my thinking, like deep worship-sharing. In the middle of this poem, though, four lines appeared that seemed out of place, not of me.

Reach over the gulf.

Connect heaven and earth.

Carry back the message:

    God is.

I have been sitting with this instruction. I sometimes hear it as that I am to "live God." I am being called to live out this love of God, to live so that God is obvious in the world through me. My inner contemplative work of loving God carries into the outer world.

I can feel myself being led to follow this instruction in work that I am doing for New England Yearly Meeting. To my surprise and with some resistance, I found myself led to clerk a working party under the care of the yearly meeting Ministry and Counsel. The working party is to help monthly meetings thresh our relationship with Friends United Meeting in the face of its discriminatory employment policy against gays and lesbians. This work is not the contemplative interior work that I thought God had in mind for me this year. The concern is contentious with deeply held beliefs and feelings on both sides. Although I am a gay man, my leading does not have to do with any position on the concern. Rather, I feel called to hold the process in God's care, to anchor Friends in remembering that we are seeking God's will, not ours. How do we love each other in spite of deep differences on particular issues? How do we witness the Truth as we see it while loving God in others? This leading feels like a way to "live God," a way to anchor us as Friends, a way to carry back the message: God is. I pray that God will give me the strength and grace to love God by serving in this way. That will only be possible if I focus only on my love for God.

Phil Fitz *is a member of Northampton (MA) Meeting. He is currently in the School of the Spirit Spiritual Nurturers Program.*

    (*What Canst Thou Say?* February 2005
    "Loving God with Our Whole Being")

A Spirit-Led Fast

Peg Morton

In the wee hours of a Monday morning this July, the thought swam into my brain that I could devote the week to a fast and vigil on the steps of Oregon's state capitol in Salem, in support of raising revenue for human services.

I had for many months been involved in the movement to stop the war in Iraq. Meanwhile, Oregon legislators had been enclosed since January inside their marble walls attempting to balance a much-diminished state budget. A small group of mostly disabled people had been trying to raise the attention of the public, and the legislators, to the suffering and instability that was already occurring due to loss of medication and services to thousands of low-income Oregonians. This group approached many of us in the peace movement, asking us why we were not involved in their struggle. I am retired from the mental health profession. As a war tax resister, I am very aware of the billions of tax dollars that go for current and past military spending, leaving very little for human needs. Touched by the descriptions of what was happening to disabled people in our state, I began traveling to Salem with the group.

The germ of my idea to fast came from the fact that another woman, Michelle Darr, had fasted, vigiled, and camped on the same steps for 56 days and nights during the Iraq war. My heart leapt up and my spirit opened at my idea. There was never any question about a decision. That it might be unsafe to camp out on the steps never occurred to me. I called some Fellowship of Reconciliation friends in Salem that morning to inform them of my plan and ask for assistance. When I arrived two days later for an action, there were Michelle and some of her friends, ready to camp out with me and support me during the following week!

What was happening to me was a spiritual leading. My experience has been that most of the time, but not always, when there was a true spiritual leading, the way opened for it to work out. That was what happened with this fast and vigil. No leading comes out of the blue. For me, this was a part of a long-term leading to make fasting, as a bodily, spiritual and political discipline, an integral part of my life. As an activist with a very full life, this leading represented a pull in a different direction. I couldn't fast and organize!

The leading has unfolded only gradually, while I have waited for my heart and mind to inform me of each next step. I have joined others in day-long fasts around political events, and engaged in a 5-day juice-broth fast on the first anniversary of 911. A few years ago, I joined a national two-week fast to close the SOA (Army School of the Americas), and, last year, joined some Dominican sisters at the Fort Benning SOA demonstration in a 36-hour water fast.

I began this summer's fast and vigil to raise Oregon state revenue for human services exactly one week following its conception. As I sat there, I was joined and supported by an ongoing stream of people, quite a few of them Friends and/or members of the Salem Fellowship of Reconciliation. They came to sing in the rotunda (and in one case, to open a House session by singing uninvited!), to stand holding signs and participate in a couple of news conferences and rallies, to make personal visits of friendship, to bring supplies, and to camp out to protect me at night. The nights were incredibly beautiful, with cool, clear air and skies in the intensely hot weather, and glimpses of the new moon.

Many disabled people were among my supporters, taking turns sleeping near me and telling me their stories. One of my new friends was living with AIDS. He was removed from the Oregon Health Plan because, they said, he had not made a payment. It turned out that he had, but the information had not been transferred from the computer to the records. Meanwhile, he was off his medications for two months. Another of my supporters informed me that he too had been removed from the Oregon Health Plan. He lived with Post Traumatic Stress Syndrome, was subject to panic attacks, and feared being around people. He was homeless.

Media coverage for this fast and vigil was extensive and an important part of publicizing an issue that had not been receiving adequate attention and grassroots support. A lobbyist said, "You are lobbying outside while we are lobbying inside." A disabled woman living with mental illness said, "I do not have a voice in there. You are providing a voice for me." Countless people have since told me that they held me in their prayers and their thoughts. It became clear to me that we were doing the right thing at the right time, increasing public awareness and involvement. While I was there, I was able to make contact with several Eugene area and other legislators. Those personal contacts were important also.

It was exciting to me that two other women decided to fast and vigil on the same steps, consecutively. We were able to have an ongoing presence for three weeks and two days.

When I returned home, the legislature was still in session, struggling. More participants in the Eugene community joined the grassroots struggle. There was a carefully planned news conference, followed by a line into a cyber-café, where we each could enter letters to our legislators on a computer. And there were many letters to the editor.

The legislators finally voted the budget and went home. Although services are still greatly diminished in Oregon, a fair number of Republicans had joined the Democrats to pass a budget that would restore many services. Taxes were raised to accomplish this. We were informed by some legislators that our presence was helpful in keeping them there, struggling for better results. Now there is a tax initiative that could well undermine these legislative accomplishments. So the work continues.

Meanwhile, each of us was personally influenced in one way or another by our actions. As I sat there on my juice-broth fast, in the shade of the north side of the building, my body cleansed itself out. With expanses of quiet between visitors, my soul was cleaned out also, and welcomed the Spirit to flow through me and out in a way that had never happened to me before. I gave more fullness of attention to those who spoke to me than is usually the case. I thought, "This is the way I am meant to be."

I have thought of legislators, enclosed in their marble buildings, dealing with financial figures, and of corporate executives, inside their glass walls, walled away from the suffering, the real stories of real people.

And now my question is: To what extent am I, and perhaps other good people working for justice and peace, separated from the people and groups for which we try to advocate, separated by the demand of our jobs and families, and in activist time spent in front of computers, on the phone, in meetings, inside the walls of our all too homogeneous faith communities? Yes, organizing work is important, but do we, or how can I, find the space to be "the way I am, and we are, meant to be," to be more fully human? I am determined to slow down, to leave more space in my life, to spend more time walking, in reflection, and meeting and knowing people from diverse backgrounds. Can I do that and not swing back into my beloved old patterns? That is the question.

Peg Morton, *age 73, is a devoted member of the Eugene (Oregon) Friends Meeting.*

(*What Canst Thou Say?* May 2004 "Guidance")

Living in My Hands

James Baker

Massage seems to be a kind of prayer—a physical prayer. For me, there's something about touch that is critically important to life. Let me describe how I began to do massage.

I was feeling lonely. I was longing for something. I thought to myself, "What do I want? I want to touch someone who wants to be touched, and I want to be touched." I had always lived through my hands. I thought of being a photographer or a sculptor. But for once in my life I did something straightforward. I got some oil and a roll of paper towels, and I started rubbing anyone who would hold still. I started with my family, then my church and other friends. I took a couple of early, really helpful massage courses.

When I started massage, I loved the feel of touching a body, any part of it, with oil on my hands. I was *in* my hands. I don't know any other way of describing it. Once I have touched someone I never forget it. Working with clay was something like massage for me. It was creating something new. Except that a living person was more satisfying to me. When I did massage it felt as if I was re-creating whoever I was massaging.

Very early on I realized that, when I was massaging, I needed to be a rigorously safe place for that person. If my intentions changed during the massage I was betraying my own inner ideal. That helped purify, for want of a better word, my hand-prayer for that person's well-being. At retreats I became the massage person—instead of going to lectures I massaged people.

After long seeking I was led to my true life, understanding the laws of healing. Later I was fortunate to be able to work with Dora Kunz. With her I experienced Therapeutic Touch as energy sensing and transference, rather than direct touch. I have learned to send love and healing by the combination of the highest intention and purpose I can manage. I try to allow my deepest self to be a conduit for the highest I know of Divine Love to flow through my hands. I think whatever healing is possible is a result.

Once, I saw a forlorn little newborn baby, whom I could not touch because I saw it through a nursery window. I let the Presence within me well up and flow to that child. The baby responded, looked at me, and went to sleep. On another occasion, a young woman artist talked incessantly during her massage, then suddenly said, "I feel like you are my psychiatrist," because she hadn't noticed my hands but was releasing her inner tensions. Most frequently, someone will be silent during a massage, but early on will heave a great, deep sigh. Often such a person will go into a deep sleep.

I agree with Dora Kunz, who once said, "When doing healing, people often say, 'You reach out to the other person.' That is not my way. My way is first to go inside, find your center, then, *from that*, reach out." When doing healing massage, I experience what William James in *Varieties of Religious Experience* refers to as one's center of personal energy. If the center has a place, it is somewhere in the upper center core of my body. But it flows through my hands in massage, and out from my body, as to that baby. For me there is also joy involved, a deep peace at my center when I massage. Perhaps that is the kind of peace Jesus promised—what Teilhard de Chardin meant when he said, "Joy is the infallible sign of the presence of God."

James Baker *is retired and helping to care for his littlest grandchildren. He remembers fondly his beloved Downers Grove Meeting in Illinois.*

(*What Canst Thou Say?* August 2009 "Body Prayer")

Stretch Out Your Hands

Maurine Pyle

For several years I rented a bedroom in my condominium to a boarder. Todd wasn't just any old boarder. I had met him at our Quaker meeting one Sunday morning where he had gone seeking solace for his troubles. Somehow his life got tangled up with mine. That is how God does it. A simple hello eventually leads to someone living in your back bedroom. What brought Todd eventually to my door was a deep desire for spiritual direction, something he had longed for all of his life. I became his guide and mentor for three years while he struggled.

One night at the dinner table as we were enjoying his good home cooking, I noticed that he was very sad, more sad than usual. When I inquired, he told me his friend Betty, an Internet buddy from Colorado, was quite ill with breast cancer. I suggested that we sit and pray for Betty after dinner.

As we centered into silence I immediately and clearly heard a word—fragrance. I held onto this word until our meditation had ended. I knew exactly where to go next—Song of Songs, Chapter I. Although I rarely touch this book of the Bible, I quickly found the verse I was looking for: "When your name is spoken aloud, it is like a spreading perfume." I told Todd that this was a message for Betty. He was used to my odd intuitive ways so he immediately went to send her an email message. Her reply came in an instant: "Bless Maurine. That quotation was cross-stitched by a friend of mine and sits framed on my mantle next to my children's pictures."

How did I know? I did not know. I am willing to bear a message and this one was stunningly specific. What did it mean? To me it meant God was sending a direct blessing to Betty to comfort her. I was simply the messenger.

In the Book of John 21:18 Jesus says to Peter, "I tell you solemnly as a young man, you fastened your belt and went about as you pleased. But when you are older you will stretch out your hands and another will tie you fast and carry you off against your will." Afterwards, Jesus said, "Follow me."

I first stretch out my hands and then I follow where I am led. That is how some miracles are worked.

Maurine Pyle *of Lake Forest Friends Meeting, Illinois, is servant leader, otherwise known as clerk, of Illinois Yearly Meeting.*

(*What Canst Thou Say?* May 2004 "Guidance")

Prophecy Isn't Easy

Rhonda Pfaltzgraff-Carlson

During an opening in 2005, I heard God telling me I was to be a spiritual teacher. I wasn't sure what that meant, but I associated it with being a prophet. Once I could no longer ignore that call passively or actively, I endeavored to live into it. Jeremiah was the prophet that rose in my mind and experience, so I learned as much as I could about Jeremiah. However, my sense of the calling and my study of Jeremiah did not prepare me for having a prophetic vision.

One night in May of 2010, I was crying my heart out. I had stumbled into the emptiness that had been buried inside me since the day I was born. After about 45 minutes of unbroken wailing, the words "corporations are dinosaurs" flashed into my mind. Hearing those words surprised me, as I had been lost in the feeling of being bereft of care. I did not have the energy to ask God for more understanding, but sensed that God desired the extinction of corporations.

While I felt that this was a significant revelation, I did not share it publicly. The implications of it were antithetical to the direction that I was going in my life. I was pursuing a master's degree in theology, hoping to integrate it with my doctorate in Industrial-Organizational Psychology. I wanted to help convey the importance of morality to businesses, most of which would be corporations. This revelation did not support the work I had been intending to do. I had wanted to help corporations be better, not tell them they needed to change an essential aspect of their structure.

On August 11, 2011, when Mitt Romney at the Iowa State Fair said, "Corporations are people, my friends," I knew I could no longer keep quiet. I wrote an articled titled "Corporations are Dinosaurs, My Friends" and published it my monthly meeting's newsletter.

Soon after the article was published, I was asked by the Adult Education Committee to lead a second hour. Subsequently, during the Occupy Wall Street movement, "Corporations are Dinosaurs" became a protest sign held by someone who had read the article. Also, St. Timothy's Episcopal Church shared the article on their web site while Walter Brueggemann, an Old Testament Bible scholar, was presenting a seminar on the book of Jeremiah there.

This message is still hard for me to hear. Even while many people might resonate with the sense of it, I believe that we are still too caught up in corporate influences to allow them to go the way of dinosaurs. Corporations are so integrated into our way of life that we feed them unknowingly. Corporate influence is preventing our political system from implementing policies that could help mitigate the devastation of life due to climate change.

This message is a wake-up call intended to help us perceive the extent to which our social structures are misaligned with gospel order. Like Jeremiah articulating God's critique of Israel's conduct:

"I brought you into a plentiful land to eat its fruits and its good things. But when you entered you defiled my land, and made my heritage an abomination.

"The priests did not say, 'Where is the Lord?'; those who handle the law did not know me; the rulers transgressed against me; the prophets prophesied by Baal, and went after things that do not profit." (Jeremiah 2:7-8)

This message is calling us to know God inwardly, so that that Life can become manifest in our social structures. If all of us would listen to and follow the Inner Teacher, we could be a *"priestly kingdom and a holy nation"* (Exodus 19:6).

Rhonda Pfaltzgraff-Carlson's *regular spiritual practice is a loose combination of Centering Prayer and Rex Ambler's* Experiment with Light, *which she has practiced regularly for over five years. In addition to waiting on God, she cares for her husband and children. The article "Corporations are Dinasaurs, My Friends" is in the* Community Companion *9-2011 issue, pp. 7-9 <communityfriendsmeeting.org/home/newsletter/cc>.*

(*What Canst Thou Say?* February 2013 "Prophetic Vision")

Finding God in Our Challenges

To love at all is to be vulnerable. Love anything, and your heart will certainly be wrung and possibly be broken. If you want to make sure of keeping it intact, you must give your heart to no one, not even to an animal. Wrap it carefully round with hobbies and little luxuries; avoid all entanglements; lock it up safe in the casket or coffin of your selfishness. But in that casket—safe, dark, motionless, airless—it will change. It will not be broken; it will become unbreakable, impenetrable, irredeemable.... The only place outside Heaven where you can be perfectly safe from all the dangers and perturbations of love is Hell.
—C.S Lewis

Choosing a life with God doesn't create a broad highway through life. Instead, we may still find ourselves in a thicket often as not, but now we have a Guide, Teacher, Trail Marker. Thankfully, our authors' experiences suggest an expanded concept of God as Comforter, Companion, Guide.

Mariellen Gilpin chooses God rather than the attractions of mental illness; Rosemary Blanchard looks back at her life and realizes she is a chick pecking at her shell. Jay Mittenthal devotes this chapter of his life to undoing his ego, and Eileen Bagus realizes her sensitivity is not a problem but an asset. Marty (Verna) Neidigh's life is saved by a mysterious Stranger, and Linda Lee considers the irony of teaching old ladies the art of self-defense. Anne Highland needs a can opener to survive a canoe trip, and is led through wilderness to a can opener. Pam Melick has an intuition that she must save her father's life—and does so.

Mary Kay Glazer learns to sing in worship even though she knows she is not a singer; Heidi Blocher expects to grieve the death of her sister, but instead feels moved to a dance of celebration. Jeanne Kimball chooses to face the darkness as a child of Light. Viv Hawkins found a growing faith in God in India.

Eric Sabelman shares his moment of getting stuck in a state of prayer. Barbara Clearbridge feels very alone, but senses God's presence is as real as friendship. Janis Ansell shares her conversation with God.

Jean Roberts finds her mystic awareness called mental illness by the doctors, and chooses to say as little as possible in order to pass for normal. Ruth Stillwell pens a sonnet about arthritis. Faith Paulsen sees the image of God in her disabled son. Carol Roth receives a divine warning and prevents a massive chain reaction accident. Jennifer Frick knows intuitively that her mother-in-law will die—and because she knows, she can be with her father-in-law; and Wendy Clarissa Geiger has a vision of a sane future devoid of nuclear weapons.

Walk with our authors as they negotiate life's challenges with God by their side.

God, It's You I Love

Mariellen Gilpin

Some years ago I was in a period of spiritual ferment because I realized I could not say I loved God. I had faith in God; I prayed a lot. But I couldn't detect that I loved God. A small child loved whoever loved him or her; it was a reflected love, a love that was a natural response to being loved. I knew God loved me, so why couldn't I say, "I love you, God"? I tried, but I couldn't honestly feel love, so I said, "I'm sorry, God. I can't say it yet. I'll do it as soon as I can."

During that period I was awakening in the night, fighting the hallucinations that are part of my mental illness. I was trying to train myself to choose not to hallucinate. One evening after dinner at a friend's house I realized I was anticipating going home and having a good hallucination. I biked home saying, "Now God, I understand I have to learn to be sane. But please, don't make it more than I can fight tonight."

I woke up at two o'clock and my physical symptoms were at their most seductive, in effect saying, "Come play with me!" I was torn, but then I rolled over in bed, slammed my fist into my pillow—quietly, since my husband was asleep—and said, "God, it's you I love, not these phenomena!" And I rolled over and went to sleep.

I learned that love was not just a feeling, not primarily anyway. Feeling was how we first found out about love. But it was also a series of decisions—choices—behaviors. And most important, love was a way of seeing.

***Mariellen Gilpin**, is a member of the WCTS editorial team. She celebrates the many ways God has helped her deal with mental illness.*

(*What Canst Thou Say?* February 2005 "Loving God with Our Whole Being")

Like a Chick Pecking at Its Shell

Rosemary Ann Blanchard

I was a young woman, getting ready to graduate from a small Catholic women's college. It was a time of giddy anticipation, coupled with a fear of the unknown. My classmates and I were at the end of our undergraduate experience, getting ready to move on to whatever life had waiting for us. What I remember the most is that we were like chicks still in the egg, pecking at the shell to emerge into who knew what.

I feel like that's where I am all over again, as I grow older and my body wears out while my spirit is still being born. I have made peace with the injury I did to my body, more than 23 years ago, in an automobile accident that almost killed me. I've made peace with it, but I still haven't got used to it. I'm still surprised when I wake up and start to spring out of bed and can't. For more than 23 years, getting up has been a slow, achy process for me. I still have, somehow, inside me a lively young woman without physical limits who's pecking at the shell of her limitations, trying to emerge.

Maybe that's where we all are, to one degree or another. My theology doesn't go any deeper than that. Theology was my curse in college—I was so good at it that it almost ate my faith. I could write an essay on just about any proposition, and I wrote myself into a state of nonbelief.

Over the next several years after I graduated, I relaxed into a comfortable agnosticism, until I surprisingly found myself called, inwardly, toward a spiritual Something that wouldn't let me go, even though I told myself I didn't believe in it. Haltingly, I began a timid return to something like prayer through the theology-free guidance of a Quaker meeting, located across the street from my house. My Friends encouraged me to wait on the Spirit and not worry about what it all meant. A dear Friend, Henry, the greeter who had met me the first time I ventured to cross the threshold into Meeting, assured me that the Way would open in its own good time and that if I was supposed to be there, eventually the reasons would become clearer to me. I began to relax and trust the Something that seemed to be calling me toward some approximation of worship. I began to think that maybe Henry was right, and I didn't need to construct a theological stance to explain to myself what I was doing.

One day I needed more faith than I had regained yet. I was preparing for surgery because of a cyst-like growth on an ovary, and my doctor told me that it was virtually impossible that a young woman of my age could have an ovarian cancer. He didn't know how hollow his words were for me. My younger sister's fiancé, a boy of 21, had recently died of non-Hodgkins lymphoma after a short and terrifying illness. I knew more than I cared to about young people dying of cancer.

So I was pretty much on my own, and too new at worship to trust prayer. I lay in the hospital the night before the surgery, unmedicated by choice, and seeking to breathe and center myself into a place of peace. Peace came. I don't know how. I don't know from Whom or What. But, I do know that peace came.

Almost as if there was someone speaking to me, I heard/felt/experienced the question,

"So, what has your life been so far? Is it something that should have happened, or has it been some kind of dirty trick?"

Within myself, I answered: "No, it hasn't been a mistake or a bad joke. Life is good. My life has been good, even with all the things that have happened in it."

"Well then," said/breathed/expressed the Presence, "why would any of the rest of it be bad? Why would you be given something good if it was only to take it away with something bad? Do you really believe I would play that kind of a game with you?"

"No." I answered. But, as the sense of Presence was receding, I called out in spirit, "But, I still don't know what happens. I still don't understand it!"

One last echo: "You don't need to understand it. You just need to trust what you already know, what you've already seen."

I cry as I write about this, because I knew then that it was true. And, even as my beliefs have gone up and down and I've grown wary of just about anything that human beings say about God, I've never lost the Faith that it was true. This is a Faith that is grounded in Trust more than in Belief. To come into existence, to live, is good. Good! Whatever follows from having come into existence is also Good and will be Good.

Rosemary Blanchard *is a member of Albuquerque Friends Meeting and a frequent attender at Sacramento Friends Meeting. Her practice is spottier than she wishes it were, "and more Spirit-led than I have any right to expect. Any more than that and I'd be veering closer to theology than I'm comfortable with, to say nothing of sounding like less of a slacker than I actually am."*

(*What Canst Thou Say?* June 2012 "Disabilities")

Undoing the Ego

Jay Mittenthal

With a controlling mother and a distant father, I learned to be a control freak and an approval junkie. To keep a semblance of control and to get a modicum of approval, I tried to become self reliant. I focused on what I could do well—on schoolwork, where critical and judgmental evaluation is applauded. However, choosing to *do,* over choosing to *be,* draws a veil over Spirit, *I am.* Trying to control breeds fear and guilt. Since control is impossible, the inevitable failure breeds frustration and anger. In judgment and avoidance of my parents, I became alienated from them. Eventually my angry outbursts ended my first marriage when I was 50.

Alone and afraid, not wanting to live a solitary, isolated old age as my parents did, I sought help. I met with a faculty colleague who was unmarried, reputed to be an outstanding teacher, and known to be a recovering alcoholic. At our lunch it was clear that we responded with addiction to similar histories. He chose alcohol; I chose control and approval. He explained that his path to recovery, the twelve steps of Alcoholics Anonymous, worked for people with hundreds of kinds of addiction. He agreed to become my sponsor. In many afternoon meetings we worked through the steps.

I came to believe in God again, after being agnostic for decades. I became a Quaker and a student of *A Course in Miracles*. I came to understand that my parents and I had developed illusory images of ourselves and the world. In our childhoods we developed an ego—a set of beliefs and expectations—that enabled us to survive but that cloaked Spirit. (EGO = Edging God Out.) Gradually I felt release from the ego. Bicycling home from these meetings, I often wept with gratitude and relief.

A dialogue in "Monty Python and the Holy Grail" summarizes my recovery:

Peasant: Well, she turned me into a newt!

Knight: A newt?

Peasant: [meekly after a long pause] ... I got better.

To go beyond this and ask the role of Spirit is the realm of conjecture. Surely the thoughts and feelings that directed me to my sponsor and sustained me as we worked the steps were grace. Grace also led me to meet Terri, with whom I'm happily married. Am I still addicted to control and approval? Yes, though less so (with large fluctuations) over time. I don't have to keep them under control if I relinquish control to God every day. I lose peace and become angry when I feel unheard or judged. But, I recognize that those feelings almost always arise from a misunderstanding. Reflection and reading the *Course* help to restore my perspective, allowing me the release of forgiveness. On the whole, I can say that I live in grace.

Jay Mittenthal *is a member and former clerk of Urbana-Champaign Meeting, Illinois. He and Terri Mittenthal open their home to spiritual pilgrims every Thursday night.*

(*What Canst Thou Say?* May 2010 "Addition and Grace")

Sensitivity: Asset or Problem?

Eileen Bagus

When I was growing up, my sensitivity was considered more of a defect than an asset by my family. I cried easily and felt emotions to the core of my being. If my parents were fighting or angry with me, I would run to my bedroom and hide behind the door. It was difficult for me to deal with the rough and tumble side of school mates. My mother would throw up her hands and call me "*empfindlich*," a German word that means roughly "overly sensitive, lacking a thick enough skin to cope with life."

Pets and plants were my friends, the gentle companions that helped me survive childhood. My sister and I dressed our toy fox terrier, Frisky, in doll clothes and carried her around in a small clothes basket. We had an aquarium on the kitchen counter filled with assorted fish. I liked to put my finger in the water and stroke the sides of the black mollys as they came to the surface to feed. Over the years assorted parakeets and canaries made their homes at our house. My favorite was an old white canary called Betty given to us by my godmother. I loved to hold her on my finger, talk to her and pet her on her back. She trusted me to put her on her back in the palm of my hand and give her little sips of water from a tiny children's play spoon. If someone had called me a tree hugger then, I would have considered it an accurate compliment.

As I grew older, I began to learn some skills for managing my sensitivity. In college it was often possible to choose those with whom I spent my time, and I began actually liking people and being able to open my tender self to some deep human relationships. Profound sensitivity allows one to open one's heart and mind to another with few barriers and, if circumstances provide enough protection, touch souls. It has the potential to make relationships divine or deeply wounding. I have had both and am still learning how to sort my human encounters so that I am not completely open all the time.

It's hard for a highly sensitive person to survive happily without some training. A number of avenues have provided me with awareness and skills for self-management. Because I love the natural world so much, I majored in biology and minored in chemistry. A scientific background allows me to both immerse myself in an experience and at the same time partially stand back and observe it with as much objectivity as I can muster at the time. (This works better for some things than others: good for questioning the para-normal events which sensitive people are prone to experience, seldom useful in love relationships where I am usually as fully present as I am able to be.)

Observing an experience, or what Buddhists would call "playing the Witness," takes some of the edge off total involvement in the world for a person with highly receptive sensors, reducing the pain of continuous over-stimulation.

Many sensitive people suffer from confusion about what source is producing a stimulus. You might, for example, at times hear a voice at a distance as clearly as someone talking beside you. Such an experience can challenge your sense of reality and make you, or others to whom you describe it, think you are going crazy, a schizophrenic hearing voices. You might find it difficult to be in social situations, as I did in my childhood, because they provide too much input. Worst of all, you may become seriously ill because your body cannot process and integrate the great variety of stimuli that is coming in to you.

One of my best teachers of how to transform sensitivity from a liability to an asset is a highly sensitive woman who developed crippling arthritis when she was in her thirties. As she learned to accept, understand, refine and control her great range of stimulus inputs, her body gradually healed. She is now a nationally known intuitive counselor.

Following are some of her suggestions to me.

1. Do not subject yourself to too much negative news in newspapers or television. The reason is that you may absorb the news far more deeply than an average person, possibly feeling the pain of others as if it were your own. I had to stop working as a therapist because I could not separate myself sufficiently from the pain of my clients and became overwhelmed by the cumulative effect.

2. Guard your choices of movies and reading matter, as you may find yourself blending into the story. If you do blend, your body will feel almost as much as if you were undergoing the same events. This can be very wearing. Once, as I watched the movie *A Star Is Born*, I felt myself dying along with one of the characters. You don't need to die on a regular basis!

3. Nourish yourself with positive surroundings and people. They will strengthen your total mind-body-emotions-spirit.

4. Laugh often.

5. Spend time in nature or with pets. The unconditional love of a pet helps love to resonate in you and keeps you in balance.

6. Meditate. It helps a sensitive person in many ways. Initially it clears the mind of most thoughts and thereby soothes raw nerves. At an intermediate level it helps to prioritize thoughts and may aid in discriminating between ordinary and paranormal information, or in sifting major/critical/creative ideas from a buzz of thinking. At its deepest level, it removes all thought and allows the person to reside in a state of open, pregnant awareness—the healing peace of God. In meditation the sensitive person may receive guidance that allows her to act in a very precise way with minimal wear and tear on her vulnerable system. I practice Transcendental Meditation.

These suggestions may sound like escapism, but they are not. They can keep the sensitive person balanced and functioning—the best way she can be happy and of benefit to others. As I grow healthier, I can make more productive use of my intuition.

Eileen Bagus *is a Friend, wife, and mother. Retired from teaching philosophy, practicing social work, selling real estate, and rehabbing houses, she now spends much of her free time in Quaker ministry and playing with her dog, April.*

(*What Canst Thou Say?* February 2004 "Open and Tender")

My Guardian Angel?

Verna Neidigh

Early on the day of the Blizzard of 1978, when I left my home to keep an appointment less than an hour's drive away, I fully expected to be home by noon, long before the predicted snowstorm. Instead, by 11:00 AM I was struggling past ditched cars, trying to drive from Knox, Indiana, through heavy snow to reach US 30, a distance of about seven miles. After an hour I finally turned east onto US 30 into a white-out of blinding snow. Nevertheless, as long as I could follow the faint red taillights of the semi-truck ahead, I felt somewhat safe.

However, when the red lights disappeared, so did the safe feeling. Not knowing what else to do, I kept on driving, creeping along in the zero visibility. Fearful questions popped into my mind. Would my car be rear-ended? Would a truck hit the car? Was I even on the highway? Where was I, anyway? What should I do? No answers came until from deep inside me, a silent voice commanded, *Stop*! I stopped the car.

Before I could bundle up in my emergency blanket and otherwise prepare for what might be a long wait, a youngish, bearded man appeared at my window. Although the man startled me, I wasn't frightened, perhaps because he reminded me of my younger son John, beard and all. Even his pickup truck was similar to John's. Therefore, when the man couldn't make himself heard through my window, and I wasn't about to lower the window to the blizzard's fury, I motioned for him to come around the front and into the car.

As we sat beside each other, he told me where we were: on the left shoulder of the eastbound lanes. He also explained that the Grovertown Truck Stop was just north of us, across the median and two westbound lanes. Furthermore, he knew where we could safely cross the median and westbound lanes.

I'm not sure which of us drove my car across to the truck stop. However, I do recall soon entering the truck stop's dining room, staring around at the roomful of men. With great relief I saw a lone lady anxiously beckoning to me from a booth. Delighted to join her, I learned that she'd already been stranded there for two hours. When by evening all of us were still stranded, I asked for a room for the night. Only one was available, with a double bed for us two ladies. In the morning the way was clear for us both to drive to our respective homes.

What about my youngish benefactor? All I know is that after we reached the truck stop, I saw him no more. At the time, I thought it wonderfully strange that he'd known where we were and that he'd helped me to my truck stop haven. In recent years, I've come to believe he was one of God's messengers, an angel. I'm at peace and in awe with that belief.

Note: In 1998 I contacted the truck stop for the names and phone numbers of any employees who were there that day and night. I was given one waitress, Vi Hanselman. According to Vi, she and the other employees on duty then were stranded for three days, without relief, except to take turns sleeping. As of January of 2008, Vi was still employed at the Grovertown Truck Stop.

The other day, as Bob and I rode past the truck stop, we couldn't help but notice the access road my angel and I possibly took to cross the median. However, I cannot imagine my driving across the median anywhere, obliterated as it was by the blizzard. Neither would it have been practical for my angel to have exchanged seats with me to do the driving. I do know I ended up in the truck stop with my car in the parking lot, leaving my benefactor there, with his pickup truck on the other side of the highway. Ah, sweet mysteries of God! I also noticed that the road curved up ahead. If I'd continued driving without seeing at all where I was going...well, I'm so thankful for that stop command!

Verna (Marty) Neidigh *is a member of South Bend, Indiana, Friends Meeting. Hard of hearing, she works to improve services for other hard of hearing people.*

(*What Canst Thou Say?* November 2008 "Angels")

Escape Plan

Linda Caldwell Lee

Some come to the church in a van, most drive.
Couples lean on each other,
   gray-haired women ease arthritic knees onto the nearest chairs.

The young instructor needs no microphone.
He tells sixty-six old people to practice in pairs.
Go for the throat. Palm open, fingers spread,
   shout as you hit, protect your face.
Practice this a thousand times.

Even a small hand is large
   when stretched from thumb to index finger.
A cane is a stick. A walker is a weapon.
Even old women can surprise a sociopath. Strike first.

You who are as sheep in the field
   must become fierce dogs against the wolves. Be ready.
Hit the side of his neck. If you miss whack the ear.
Practice running away.

Outside a red maple burns, oak leaves fly against the windows.
Soon we will all go home to pray for Jane whose throat was slit,
   for Monika who was strangled,
   for the policeman who would give his life for yours,
   for those who would as soon grind your grandmother as eat a burger.

© 2006. All rights reserved. Reprinted with permission. **Linda Lee** is a former editor of WCTS, and a member of First Friends Meeting, Indianapolis, Indiana.

(*What Canst Thou Say?* May 2008 "Transforming Conflict")

The Can Opener

Anne C. Highland

We forgot to pack the can opener. We never understood how the Swiss army knife got left behind. All we had was my little pocketknife, good enough for making shavings to start a fire, but not capable of opening our cans of food. We were the only campers on a remote lake, separated from civilization by a good day's paddling.

I made an inventory; we had enough packaged food to survive: gorp, oatmeal, naked rice, a bit of fresh fruit. But eating would not be a pleasure without the canned food.

During the next day, when we never left camp because of the rain, I sat in my hammock sheltered under a couple of ponchos, watching the rain sweep across the lake. As the hours went by, I felt my mind being washed clean by the rain, becoming translucent. And toward evening the Light came through. As the dinner hour approached, I knew, and I told Virgil, if we paddled down the lake to the portage, and walked the portage trail to the next lake, at the far end of the trail we would find a can opener. In my mind's eye I saw campers on the shore of the next lake.

"Yes, but how did you know?" Virgil would ask later.

At the end of the half-mile portage trail we came out onto the shore of the next lake, carrying our cans in our cooking pots. But there was no one in sight, nor was there a campsite within view. I looked inward for guidance. "Let's wait a bit," I said. As I lifted my head, a canoe came into sight around the point, but it was paddled by two young men in bathing suits. No pockets there for a Swiss army knife. They beached their canoe near us. They carried hatchets; they had come for firewood.

We explained our predicament. "Wait a few minutes while I go back to camp. It's just around that point. I'll bring you a can opener," said the older of the pair.

When he returned he seemed empty-handed because what he carried was so small. It was a flat piece of aluminum no larger than my thumb. "Take it," he said. "It's both a can opener and an emergency spoon. Someone gave it to me when I needed it. And now it's yours for as long as you need it."

I still carry it in my briefcase, not because I need to open cans with it, but because it helps me remember we live within a Mystery.

Anne C. Highland *is a clinical psychologist in private practice in Philadelphia. She attends Gwynedd Meeting. She is preparing a book of vignettes for publication.*

(*What Canst Thou Say?* August 2004 "Knowings")

Lifesaving Questions
Pam Melick

Until I was in my twenties I ignored anything that couldn't be explained by the five senses. But in recent years knowing has sometimes meant hearing someone's thoughts before they have spoken. In other moments, I have glimpsed what was to come, followed by a deep sense of knowing. Many times, however, the knowing comes in the form of a question: "What if?" or "What would I do if?"

One such moment came in October 1995. My father underwent open-heart surgery. Because it was his second bypass, recovery was slow. Previously undiagnosed diabetes slowed his recovery even more. What should have taken weeks to heal was stretching into months. The still small voice inside said I needed to visit him. I didn't know what exactly would unfold, but I knew I needed to go.

When I arrived at the airport, I was given a seat next to the emergency exit. Then, I was asked the Question that would frame the rest of the weekend: If there were an emergency, could I open the door and help other passengers to safety? As I waited, I wrestled: What would I do if the plane crashed? How heavy was the door? Would I be able to lift it? Would I be calm enough to save lives in that type of emergency? I didn't know why, but I knew I needed to know the answers before I got to Columbus. I am happy to say the flight was uneventful. But still it nagged: *Would I be calm enough to save lives in an emergency?*

I arrived at the convalescent hospital to take my father to his apartment. My father, impatient as always, couldn't wait to leave. I checked with his nurses to see if he had eaten breakfast: he had been stubbornly refusing food for the last several weeks, dangerous for a diabetic. They assured me he had eaten. I took him home, sat him in his favorite chair, left him a little food, and went to the grocery. There was little in the house for a diabetic heart patient to eat. When I left, he was alert, rosy-cheeked, happy to be home, and assuring me he was fine.

When I returned he was slumped in his chair, too weak to lift himself. I half-carried, half-walked him to the toilet, where he became violently ill. My mind whirled. In one divine moment, the words formed clearly in my mind: sugar crash. My mind raced through everything my mother had told me about managing her diabetes. I ran to the kitchen, poured a glass of juice, and insisted he drink it. I was right. His blood sugar had dropped dangerously low.

We spent the afternoon arguing. I stubbornly insisted he eat to keep his blood sugar up. He stubbornly insisted he wasn't hungry and didn't want to

Intimacy with God

eat. My brother Ray arrived late that afternoon. I had arranged to have dinner with a friend and spend the night with her. My last words going out the door were, "Make sure he eats something every couple of hours."

Ray called me about eleven. My father had taken a painkiller and was hallucinating. Was it the pain killer or something more serious? I told Ray to dial 911. I returned to find the paramedics trying to persuade my father to go the hospital. My father had refused to eat that evening and his blood sugar was so low he could have slipped into a coma. Because he was lucid, the paramedics couldn't take him to the hospital without his consent. They suggested we do what we could to raise his blood sugar. And if he passed out, call them.

I got another glass of juice, but my father was too weak to sit up. As Ray and I worked on a better method for giving him the juice, my father started to vomit. He was on his back, and my only thought was, "Oh Lord, he's going to aspirate." I shouted for my brother to help me roll him over. I pulled from the front and Ray pushed from the back. Never stand in front of someone in the midst of projectile vomiting. We managed to get him into the bathroom again.

As we sat with him, encouraging him to drink his juice, I quietly but firmly explained to him the ramifications of the last hour. If Ray hadn't called me, if I hadn't figured out what was going on, we could have been attending his funeral, not feeding him juice. For the first time my father began truly to comprehend the consequences of refusing to cooperate with those who wanted to help him heal.

My father had left the hospital against medical advice. He ate only a little of the hospital breakfast. My brother was always an observer, not a doer. He would have been hard-pressed to handle things alone. Had one of Dad's friends taken him home instead of us, he could have died alone from insulin shock. Divine Spirit guided me that weekend. It is the only way I had the knowledge and insight precisely when needed. And beforehand, Divine guidance gave me the questions I needed most to prepare to save my father's life, twice.

I would not trade glimpses into my future for anything. But drama has lost its allure. I pray the subtle nudges become more integrated and the questions keep me on my path. I want to know where I'm being led and what I am expected to do, and I do it willingly. And I will reserve drama for those important, lifesaving questions.

Pam Melick *is Chicago Northside Meeting's representative to Illinois Yearly Meeting. She recently refinished the aged kitchen cabinets in the IYM dining room.*

(*What Canst Thou Say?* August 2004 "Knowings")

Singing a New Song

Mary Kay Glazer

When I was young, maybe around ten years old, I learned—very painfully—that I could not sing. I was sitting in a circle with a group of girls and a few adults—some sort of summer day camp. We were singing, and as we sang, we took turns singing into a tape recorder microphone. The singing was then played back so we could hear ourselves. When my voice crashed out of the little box, everyone (it seems, in my memory) laughed, made fun of the voice, and said, "*Who* is *that*???"

After decades of not singing, or singing only in my own company, or singing as quietly as possible when with others, I was quite surprised—and dismayed—when it seemed that God was asking me to sing hymns as vocal ministry in meeting for worship. I resisted for a long, long time. I think at first I thought I must be mistaken in my discernment. I certainly hoped so! Then, when the call persisted, I became afraid.

That, of course, did not stop God. Regularly in meeting for worship I felt the impulse to stand and sing. Each time, I declined the invitation—until the wedding of a dear friend. With me for almost the entire meeting for worship was a hymn. Near the end of worship, with a lot of fear and trembling, I finally stood, not knowing if my voice would freeze, if anything at all would come out of my mouth, if it would sound more like croaks and creaks than music. Not knowing until I opened my mouth and started to sing. There were some creaks, but no one gasped in horror. I don't know much about how this hymn of love was received. I only know that when I finally said yes, I felt that I was faithful, that I had done what God had asked, and I felt a sense of freedom—fear too, still, but also freedom.

Since then, I have been given other songs, mostly hymns, to sing as ministry in worship. I have not been particularly happy when that happens, but it has become a bit easier to say yes. Even when I am not asked to sing as ministry, songs of praise and worship are often in my head and on my heart during worship, and at other times, too. Music—along with silence and movement and conversations with God—is part of my inner prayer, in my day-to-day moments as well as in meeting for worship. I find that is a way back to prayer when other ways are blocked, for instance when I get too analytical or tangled up in trying to find just the right words in prayer; or when I get too distracted in my efforts in silent prayer. It is a way for me to tap into and express joy and praise in the Spirit, something that feels right but is hard for me to do. Singing releases a spiritual energy that brings me deeper into the heart of God. There is a freedom in song that is different from the freedom I find in the silence.

The sacred music in my life has not replaced the sacred silence of Quaker worship. God still invites me into the silence, and still opens me in the silence. God still uses words without music to speak to me, and sometimes no words at all. The music, like other forms of prayer, is just one way that God opens my heart to God's presence.

Sing a new song unto the Lord (Judith 16:13, Revelations 5:9)…

God has given me a new song to sing, and the singing of it has opened me to new healing, new Love, new Life—and a cherished way of worship. This musical way of worship, rather than replacing silent worship, enhances my relationship with the Eternal One. Music and silence feel integrated into the one flow of the Spirit in and through me. One leads to the other to the other to the One, so that it is all "the breath of the Spirit flowing in me."*

Thank you, oh Holy One.

from the song, "Spirit of God" by Miriam Therese Winter.

Mary Kay Glazer *lives in Ticonderoga, NY, and attends the Ticonderoga Worship Group and Middlebury, VT Monthly Meeting. She is a graduate of the School of the Spirit Spiritual Nurture Program and Shalem Institute's Spiritual Guidance Program. She is a spiritual director and retreat leader.*

(*What Canst Thou Say?* November 2010 "Silence and Music")

A Moment of Light

Heidi Blocher

An experience following the recent death of one of my sisters cast a light into my soul I felt urged to share with others.

Theres had held out with pancreatic cancer for almost three years, a blessed time for her, of inward liberation, and without overwhelming physical suffering at any time. To everyone's surprise, she reached her 70th birthday.

After receiving the news by phone, I walked downhill in the night to get the day's mail. Suddenly the woods around me turned blue: a full moon had appeared from behind the clouds, blindingly silver. "She died at full moon!" it hit me. "She wouldn't do any less. She wouldn't go before fullness was achieved!"

That fullness of light was in my soul the next morning when I woke up. The normally somber view of hemlocks beyond my window seemed pierced with bright sun and patches of strong blue. There was no heavy feeling in me at all. Instead, a great desire to dance!! I felt we should, all of us including Quakers, indeed we must, dance at funerals! Celebrate life, the life that has been, the life we still have, and the ongoingness of life beyond ourselves and those we love.

But there was something new for me in this feeling of celebration. For the first time, this fullness of joy included, quite specially, the shortness of our lives, their limitation in time. Not because life is painful (which it is; release from the valley of tears is part of this celebration) but the shortness makes it so perfect, so valuable, precious—intense. My old fondness of jewels as a child came back to me: tiny; perfectly condensed beauty and brilliance; the full intensity. I had committed myself as a child to the jewel. Like my sister with her full, brilliant moon, I would take no less.

I had been much burdened in the time of my sister's illness by a new awareness of my own mortality, the limitation of my life, and the fear that it won't be fulfilled. Now jubilation was in me for the perfection of the short, limited span given us. I saw the dance, cosmic, whirling around the globe incessantly: lives coming and going, figure yielding to figure in a continuous movement; I thought I heard the music, the cosmic joy—the joy of being just one figure in this dance, passing through, appearing briefly and disappearing in the ongoing whirl. How terrible it would be, it seemed to me, not to disappear, to deny the preciousness of both the short appearance and the ongoingness of the whole that does not need to hold on to the temporary manifestation.

I blessed my sister for her participation in the dance and for being willing to leave it, to disappear, as a figure, in its movement. How great and full my appreciation of her and her life was at this moment!

"Theres," my soul said, "I thank you. Now there is nothing but this fullness and brilliance—now your terrible sufferings of soul, and mine, including those we caused one another, are only gestures and figures of this great dance that has carried us. Now you are transfigured, your life revealed in its truth."

"Will this sense last in me?" I asked when the moment was passed. "Probably not. My legs, my heart, will grow heavy again. But I accept what is given me this morning, in fullness, as I accept the full moon, its fact, its moment, knowing it will wane, look awkward, disappear, reappear, wax again. I accept it entirely; today I am in the dance."

Looking at the window, the perfect stillness out there, I had, for a moment, a sense of pure existence. Existence not made up of this and that, but only of itself. In my mind I saw myself walking out on a frozen pond without knowing whether the thin ice would carry me or not: there was nothing out there, but I was fully, entirely engaged. There is not a part of one's being that does not participate in this act. And I longed for this pure existence, and for my life to be exactly like this. And I seemed to know that my life is like this, and the gratefulness I felt, pure gift, cannot be described.

As I lay there, savoring the quiet hour between warm flannel sheets, I came to feel myself resting in this pure existence as I had seen John resting on the breast of Jesus in a little icon I have. One can see it in the disciple's open eyes that he is listening to and feeling the heartbeat of the Master. Resting on the breast of Existence, feeling and listening to its heartbeat. I said to my sister, "Now I know this you had in your sorrowful and exalted life, and this you sought, like me: That daring, ecstatic walk on the ice, and that resting on and for the Heartbeat. At last, darling, we are sisters. It is finished."

"I feel unusually unburdened, as if nothing remained between Theres and me to clear up," I later wrote to a friend. I asked if this may owe something also to the undramatic but steady and devoted reconciliation process that had quietly evolved between us during the time of her illness, mostly by correspondence and the exchange of poetry we had held in common during our school years, which I now recognized, with deep gratefulness, had been a way for us to bond in that which is eternal. Two years before her death I went to Europe where my sister lived, to say good-bye to her, upon news that she was about to go. Mercifully, more time was given us.

Heidi Blocher *is a member of Sandwich, Massachusetts, Friends Meeting. Widely connected among Friends in both the U.S. and Europe, and long in the habit of documenting her inward experience in writing, she often shares intimately with Friends.*

(*What Canst Thou Say*? February 2009 "Gratefulness")

~~~~~~~~~~

Facing Darkness as a Child of Light
Jeanne Kimball

"Facing the Dark as a Child of Light" is a difficult phrase for me as I think of "facing" as standing up to something. In my experience there is nothing I can do to face the dark. I can't see the darkness ahead; instead I am just somehow in it. I feel it is one way the spirit works in our spiritual life and often new insight comes after a period of darkness. Light and darkness are just part of my life in the spirit.

My spiritual life is a path that goes up and down and weaves in and out. It is sometimes desert-like, stark and bleak. Then I come out into sunny, bright places with flowing water, fountains and beauty to nourish and feed me. Then there is the dark night of the spirit. It is cold and dreary and I am lost, reaching out for love and assurance, but finding only sadness and pain. Then again I come to a place of calm and peace and love. The ups and downs, the twists and turns, the darkness and light are all there as the path goes on. I meet myself on the path, sometimes in joy and sometimes in sorrow. I meet others too, those who give me support and those who seem to just be a hindrance. But God is always there in love even when my sight and sense seem dim. My faith is such that I know she is there, reaching out to me, holding me, loving me.

"In him was life, and the life was the light of men. The light shines in the darkness, and the darkness has not overcome it." (John 1:4-5)

No matter what the darkness in my spiritual life is, these verses have given me reassurance that the light is still there. The spirit does not leave me even in the times when I feel distant from God. At times I go through all the motions of prayer, going to worship, reading from the Bible and other books and there seems to be no response, no answers, no end to the darkness and despair. Somehow even in those times there is that feeling that the light is there waiting to break through the clouds.

In my experience, darkness comes at times in my spiritual life and there is nothing I have found that can stop it from coming or make it any easier at the time. All I can do is somehow continue to be faithful in prayer, attending worship and reading even though it feels like I am only going through the motions. Just as spring and new life come after a long winter, new life and joy come into my heart as well. As the poet Rabindranath Tagore says,

"Faith is the bird that feels the light and sings when the dawn is still dark."

Jeanne Kimball *attends the Florence Worship Group in Florence, Oregon, and is a member of Eugene Friends Meeting.*

(*What Canst Thou Say?* November 2004 "Darkness")

Faith to Follow: Nothing to Fear
Viv Hawkins

> *Peace I ask of thee, oh river.*
> *Peace, peace, peace.*
> *When I learn to live serenely,*
>   *cares will cease.*
> *From the hills I gather courage,*
>   *visions of the day to be,*
> *Strength to lead and faith to follow*
> *—all are given unto me.*

I reluctantly attended a "lamentations group" at my meeting where I opened my heart to the pain of the world, allowed it to stream through me, and offered it up to God. The words that spilled from me on my knees, the only posture from which I felt able to say these things, went like this, "God of Abraham, Son of David, have mercy on us for not having the faith to know we have nothing to fear."

For two years now, I have passionately sought "faith to follow." I was 50 when I became single for the second time in my adult life; I felt a wide solitude—both freeing and bereft. A few months later, I left my job after 30 years of diverse professional service; in so doing, I shed the ability to draw self-esteem from income, a title, or work that offered me stability and meaning. I reduced my possessions to those which fit in a friend's Prius (with both of us in it) so I could no longer define myself by my possessions. I gave up my apartment and accepted another friend's generous offer of hospitality; with that, I sloughed off a sense of self-sufficiency and came to know the power of mutual relations over transactions. I telephoned family and friends and wrote to those with whom I wished to make peace. I was on my way to India. I had a sense I might not return.

A year earlier, members of a Pendle Hill "Discerning Our Calls" class had found me clear to go to India. A prayer from my journal at that time asks,

"Am I willing to be re-formed, to be made anew, to die in order to live more fully? That is the question I face now. And my answer needs to be, YES! But how? How to let go of the fear involved in letting go?"

In my bones, I knew the truth in the statement of a spiritual friend who suggested that I was not going to India to "do" something but to "be done to." This pilgrimage has called up every fear I know and sent me spinning more times than I can count. Sometimes, I have felt like a kayaker capsized and bouncing off the many boulders hidden beneath the white water. Teilhard de Chardin wrote, "We can set no limits to the uprooting which is part and parcel of our journey to God."

My meeting's minute of travel for that first India trip quoted me saying, "I ready myself to freefall into God's arms... As I release material possessions, power positions, and aspects of human life which some believe offer security such as home, income, and plans for the future, I experience this as a further move into the Mystery.... Even as I feel God's enfolding, I await God's unfolding for me."

I had no idea what awaited me.

As I prepared for this I needed to learn to float down stream, feet first, and try not to clutch at the water.

One of my primary destinations was Varanasi, a city along the Ganges reputed by Hindus to be an auspicious place to die. From a respectfully distant ghat, I watched open-air cremations release the deceased's spirit and the ashes surrendered to the holy waters of the Ganges. By that quietly flowing river soon after dawn, I released my father who had been cremated by a far different process in a distant land long ago when I was 3 years old. And, a part of my spirit was freed. Throughout those three months in India, the ground of my being as I knew it, me, would be partially removed and replaced with something much firmer, a growing faith in God.

Only now, more than a year later, can I see the kenosis, the being emptied, which God perceived beginning in me. I was available in a much different sense. I was available the way a clean-swept apartment is available to its new tenant. God was moving in, sometimes at my invitation and sometimes despite my attempts at eviction.

Thanks to dear companions with whom I share mutual accountability to faithfulness, more and more we return to God—the original meaning of "repent." And, in gratitude for what I have received, I tenderly place my hands under the heads of people reticent to float in the Divine as they reluctantly lay their backs on the water and turn their hearts to the sky.

By faithfully following, in so far as I have, I touch the hem of the Infinite and glimpse the Eternal. A part of me had no idea this is what would be revealed. Another part of me knew irrevocably this belovedness of God is my inheritance as much as it is everyone's who thirsts for it.

God who is within, around, and beyond us all, thank You for the faith to follow so that we may know in our heart of hearts we have nothing to fear.

Viv Hawkins *is a member of Central Philadelphia Monthly Meeting.*

(*What Canst Thou Say?* February 2008 "Called")

Stuck in a State of Prayer

Eric Sabelman

On Saturday, on my way to work in the garden, I got stuck in a state of prayer.

I had felt it coming on: a very large, wide prayer rising up from deep inside.

It reached my conscious self, the level where I form it into words. It began:

"O, Thou...." "O, Thou...."

But there I was stuck, without the words to say the part that came next; I tried a lot of combinations and none were adequate:

"O, Thou Creator of earth and sea and sky..."

"O, Thou Giver of all gifts..."

"O, Thou God of grace and God of glory ... grant us wisdom, grant us courage for the living of each hour..."

Each was closer, but still far from complete (and the last was lifted from a hymn not my own).

I moved from one part of the garden to another, trying out new endings; in each place, I stood immobilized while searching for the right words, and got no gardening done.

All the words I know are not enough.

I came to have an appreciation for Jesus' wisdom in giving us what we call the Lord's Prayer, not for the purpose of a preacher leading his congregation in reciting it, but as practical advice should you become stuck in a state of prayer: "If you need words for your prayer and none come, you might try these. Then you can go on with whatever else you have to do."

Begin with "Our Father, Who art in heaven...," continue through "... for Thine is the Kingdom...," and you will very likely have said the words you needed.

Islam has something similar. I am told the Prophet gave his followers the 99 Names of God: "O, Thou Merciful...," "O Compassionate...," "O Light..." Say all 99, and you will very likely have said the words you needed. (I am also told Muhammad gave the 100th Name only to his camel, so that men could not claim to know everything.)

My prayer is still incomplete: "O, Thou..." leads to too many words of hope and thanks and praise to choose between. "O, Thou who knows my soul, who hears it speak what I cannot say..."

Saying this makes it feel less incomplete: I give this to you, in case you too are ever stuck in a state of prayer.

Eric E. Sabelman *gave this message in worship on January 26, 1997. He is in the process of publishing a collection of his ministries.*

(*What Canst Thou Say?* February 2011 "Prayer")

As Real as Friendship
Barbara Clearbridge (Shulamith Eagle)

This is a story about a time which was a mere five seconds in duration. I had just moved to Seattle and knew only two people. I had a bit of savings, so I decided to volunteer for the World Peace Event, a series of events happening around the world on New Year's Eve, 1986. I worked in the Seattle office full time for three months, helping to arrange our very large event at the King Dome (a football stadium). It was a huge effort by dozens of volunteers and only three paid staff people. According to the Director, I was in charge of the spirits of the volunteers. I kept things light and harmonious and moving along well, helped solve problems, and pitched in wherever there was a need.

The worldwide Peace Events would culminate with a period of silence when we would all pray for or meditate about peace, simultaneously, all over the Earth. Because this silent time turned out to be at 4:00 A.M. Seattle time, we scheduled four hours of entertainment starting at midnight. I was on quite a high from the exciting week before the event through the night itself. Our event drew several thousand people and went off quite well.

The impact on me of the whole experience was massive. I got sick the day afterwards with extreme fatigue and a high fever. It was a mighty physical and emotional crash, probably from the loss of the intense, intimate camaraderie and the adrenaline on which I'd been living. I felt alone again—no one called me or seemed to care.

For years I'd had a spiritual guide —not a human being but someone who existed on what I can only describe as an energetic level. I communicated with him by listening or writing. Now, on my fourth day in bed, all his kind words were wasted on me. I told him I wanted comfort from someone with a body. I needed to be held, to be hugged. I lay in bed, miserable, listening to his silence. Then I was hugged. Somehow I got a loving embrace from my invisible guide. Talk about unseen hands! It scared me so badly I didn't communicate with him for months! Who was it who'd told me to be careful what I asked for because I might get it?!

It's difficult to describe what the hug was like, because as soon as I actually felt something, I freaked! It felt exactly like a human person, a warm, sympathetic, dear old friend, putting his arms, filled with love, around me. I had no sense of the rest of his body—just his arms and his gargantuan, enfolding love, that carried with it feelings of respect for me and my own worthiness. I became more fully aware later—after I was over the shock of discovering that the other world I only thought I believed in was real as nails. No, better: as real as friendship.

I treasured the memory of that moment. I eventually ended up teaching workshops on how to find one's guide, and I included a way to be touched in the exercises we did. Nearly always someone has had a breakthrough and the spiritual world, once again, proves itself real.

Within a few years of this experience, I grew into a healer and medical intuitive. When I had—or have, even now—a client beyond my skills, I can borrow, so to speak, my guide's eyes. Then my vision expands until I can see what needs to be done. Sometimes, if I'm not able to provide what's needed, my guide will work through my hands. The energies I feel at those times are distinctive—different frequencies and far more powerful than what I can gather or generate. (In fact, they are so distinctive that a perceptive, longstanding client could tell when my guide began to help me.) My body could barely tolerate these energies at first, and after only a few minutes I would break out in a sweat, get dizzy, and have to let go of him. Over the years, as I've grown stronger and more skilled and grounded, he's taught me more and more and I need him much less often. Still, he always shows up when I call. At the start of sessions I always ask for help from the guides of my clients, too. Sometimes their presence and help is palpable.

People have suggested it's really some part of me that I'm accessing, but it isn't. When I've asked for proof, my guide has provided it. He's proved it again on many occasions when my students call on him without my knowing, to help them. And then there is that hug!

Barbara Clearbridge (Shulamith Eagle) *has recently moved to Vermont and now attends Burlington Friends Meeting.*

(*What Canst Thou Say?* November 2008 "Angels")

Free and Infinite

Janis Ansell

The tenth query in the Faith and Practice of my Yearly Meeting asks, "Do we endeavor to live in harmony with nature? Are we careful in our stewardship of the world's irreplaceable resources?" Each year as I hear the query read I face a dilemma, for the answer is neither simple nor easy. I accept, regretfully, that no matter how careful I am, I could be unwittingly depleting the world's resources despite intentional efforts to do otherwise.

Recently one of those *aha* moments with which God gifts me from time to time opened a new way of seeing the query and what is required of me. There is a resource, freely poured out upon all creation, which cannot be depleted—God's love. I need only be willing to receive this divine love and allow it to flow through me. To the extent I surrender to being a channel for God's love I live in harmony with God's desire that I be a co-creator in the Divine plan. At times creation seems, from my limited human perspective, to be unpleasant, ugly even, akin to suffering and death. When I am willing to experience the totality of the creative process, accepting everything that comes to me as a gift from God, then I live in wholeness even through periods my human understanding would call times of pain, struggle, or death. Realizing that relying on the infinite resource of God's love is all that is essential. This relieves me of the worry about making a bad choice or doing the wrong thing despite my good intentions. I trust God to guide me in all my actions, including those relating to stewardship of creation. As I allow myself to surrender the details of life to God's loving guidance, my way of living is changing to match my shifting inner condition. I am conscious of the food I grow, buy and consume, as well as the amount of fossil fuel used to produce and transport our food. I eat as locally as possible and endeavor to limit consumption of commercially processed foods.

God is leading me and my husband beyond the initial steps we've already taken by driving hybrid cars, installing solar hot water, using compact fluorescent light bulbs and planting a larger vegetable garden. Those steps were a good beginning that we now accept to be only an introduction to what is required of us. Now we are being nudged firmly toward a simpler life of sustainable farming. God is asking us to let go of material goods and to build a smaller, zero-energy house powered by the source of energy God has freely offered us all—the sun. God is asking us to teach others what we are learning and to model a life of simplicity, sustainability and love.

We rest in the Spirit of Love, freely available. We are committed to living faithfully in this covenant relationship with God and God's creation at Quaker Circle: A Sustainable Friends Community. Today we nurture the vision and the promise we have heard, and work toward purchasing land and beginning the building and planting. We trust God is laboring with us in ways we cannot yet see to acquire the land and to bring the workers who, like us, can do no less than obey the call to live in Love with Creation.

Janis Ansell *is a member of Rich Square Monthly Meeting (North Carolina Yearly Meeting Conservative). She completed the School of the Spirit's program "On Being a Spiritual Nurturer" in 2008 and now serves on its Board. Information about Quaker Circle can be found at <quakercirclesfc.com>.*

(*What Canst Thou Say?* February 2010
"A Covenant with Creation")

Q & A

Janis Ansell

Why me, God?
Why not you—
Who else?
What's next then?
One step and then—
one more and then . . .
Alone?
I AM with
you all ways
Where?
Toward the Light,
Follow me . . .
How can I?
With Love,
simply with Love
When?
Now, in this moment
and in the next . . .
Why me, God—why do you love me so much?
Why not you?
Who else?

Janis Ansell is a member of Rich Square Meeting, North Carolina Conservative. *"I am always in a Q&A with God, and the questions and answers are all pretty much the same, though the specifics may vary. It was questioning God as to whether there was anything on this topic that led to this poem."*

(*What Canst Thou Say?* August 2010 "Questioning")

The Less I Said
Jean Roberts

My spiritual awakening or spontaneous Kundalini experience occurred in 1984, before the change to the DSM. Even though I was given mind-altering drugs during my ten-day stay in a psychiatric facility, I was continually comforted and sustained by the energy of love. I was coming to know this love as the most powerful force, with which nothing could compete.

I was guided continuously and had no fear. In my student nurse days, I had learned a little about psychiatry, and so I knew the less I said about my experience, the sooner I would be discharged. Upon leaving, I talked with a psychiatrist who told me to stay away from the occult and anything else I didn't understand. At that time there was no explanation for what I was experiencing. I couldn't be put in a category with a label.

The change in DSM-IV described in the box below may help people avoid a pathological diagnosis and a label of mental illness.

Jean Roberts *is a member of Eastside (Washington) Meeting and North Pacific Yearly Meeting. She has been a Quaker for over 30 years and is a co-founder of* **What Canst Thou Say**? *Jean's account of her spiritual awakening can be found in Jennifer Elam's book,* Dancing with God Through the Storm, *and Jennifer's chapter in* Ways of Knowing: Science and Mysticism Today.

((What Canst Thou Say? May 2005 "Spiritual Emergence(y)*")*

An Important Addition to the *Diagnostic and Statistical Manual*
Jean Roberts

An addition or change to the Diagnostic and Statistical Manual (DSM) (the bible of psychiatrists and others in the medical field) often takes years to be accepted by the editors and added to the new edition. So in 1991, as Robert Turner, M.D. (a former member of the Kundalini Research Network), Francis Lu, M.D., and David Lukoff, Ph.D., made their submission to the fourth edition, they were prepared to have it debated a long time. Those who knew about this project were cautiously optimistic. Miraculously, the submission was accepted for publication in the DSM-IV under a non-pathological category. It appears as follows:

Religious or Spiritual Problem: This category can be used when the focus of clinical attention is a religious or spiritual problem. Examples include distressing experiences that involve loss or questioning of faith, problems associated with conversion to a new faith or questioning of spiritual values that may not necessarily be related to an organized church or religious institution.

Easy Mover
Ruth Stillwell

How easily I move at night,
Leaving my body lying flat:
In lissome leaps like a leopard light,
With supple smoothness like a cat!
Gliding glissando as on glass,
Twirling on tiptoe like a top,
I pirouette, plié and pass,
Soar like a singing lark—
    And plop!
Here I am, back on my bed,
Facing another graceless day,
No ease of movement now; instead,
I lurch and lumber my labored way,
Longing for darkness and dreams to free
The easy mover trapped in me.

Ruth Stillwell wrote this sonnet in 1990, shortly before she died. A member of the Wesley Methodist Church in Urbana, Illinois, her husband Gardiner chose a Quaker memorial because he wanted closeness with the Quakers, who loved her dearly.

(*What Canst Thou Say?* June 2012 "Disabilities")

The Blister

Faith Paulsen

Click. Clack. It was the soundtrack of my day, the sound of my five-year-old son Judah tapping his wooden toy trains together. A pot of soup simmered on the stove.

I sat at my kitchen table and picked up the dog-eared notebook Judah carried back and forth to school. That notebook. Every day like clockwork it came, its black and white marbled cover an intruder in my daily routine. My husband would be home soon. Judah and his brother Seth, two and a half years, were watching "Mr. Rogers Neighborhood" in the next room. Time to read the notebook.

Next to today's date was a sticker. "This is what I did today!" exclaimed the bright yellow happy face. "Language therapy today: He/she; I/you. Judah still confuses these words. Echolalia noted. Comments: We are trying to redirect Judah's behavior regarding unstructured free play. He has a tendency to go off on his own and become engrossed in one object, e.g. trains. He is in his own little world. He isolates himself and will not tolerate other children. Self-stimulatory behavior observed. Poor eye contact."

The clear message was this: Your son is imperfect, damaged, broken, God's mistake. Sometimes it felt as if we were locked in a nightmarish tug-of-war, me and my husband on one side, desperately pulling our son's body from the jaws of a monster. The monster was his autism.

Click. Clack. Judah wandered by, a toy train in each fist. He had chewed his turtleneck collar to shreds.

"Hi, honey." I leaned toward him, cupping his chin in my hand and twisting his face to mine. My eyes captured his and grasped them forcefully. "Judah, it's almost time for dinner." I paused, watching the blank face for signs of recognition.

It was like watching a glass gumball machine. The quarter went in, chugged its way down. Then, the gumball climbed a conveyor belt to the top of the transparent dome, and descended, sliding its way through roller-coaster turns, riding up and around and down until it plopped into the cup.

"You are having macaroni?" Judah finally said.

"You mean you would like macaroni."

"Okay."

"Okay, Judah. We can have macaroni. Will you help me?"

Again, the wait.

"Judah can help me?" he suggested.

"Judah can help me."

"Okay."

I propped him up on his tiptoes on top of the stepladder, and turned on the faucet. Together, we filled the saucepan and set it on the stove, moving the stepladder as we went along. While Judah perched next to the stove, gawking at the water, I turned to stir the soup.

"WA-A-A-A-A-A!" Face red, mouth contorted, Judah wrung his hands, his shriek exploding over the house.

I dropped the spoon, flew to him, swept him up in my arms.

"Oh, honey, are you hurt? What is it?"

He raised one trembling hand.

"Did you burn yourself?" Amidst his screams I pushed his hand under the faucet and let the cool water run over the burn. Then I used a clean dishtowel to swaddle his hand.

Judah glared at the bundle.

"It's a burn, honey. I know it hurts, but Momma will make it better."

I unwrapped the finger like a present. There it was, a new blister. My breath stuck in my throat.

"A tissue!" he screamed.

"A tissue? What for?"

"Wipe it off! Wipe it off!"

"Judah, no, it's a blister. Part of your own skin. It doesn't come off."

"Take off the Band-Aid!"

"It's not a Band-Aid. It doesn't come off. It's a kind of boo-boo and it will get better soon." I touched the blister to my lips.

He sniffed.

I gathered him up in my arms, wrapped myself around my son's bony body. Judah needed my reservoir of calm; I dipped into it with both hands.

He said nothing and did not return my embrace.

And then I realized. I'd said it myself. The blister was part of his own skin—like his autism. His chewed-up shirt, his gnawed fingernails, his confused pronouns, his tantrums, were all part of him. They wouldn't come off. They were woven into his gentle nature, inseparable from the presence I saw in those unfathomable hazel eyes. I could almost picture the gears, lifts and pulleys running the colorful mechanism of his mind.

His question landed with its familiar plunk. "You are playing with trains?"

"No, honey. You, Judah, you want to play with trains." I pointed to him.

He looked down at my finger touching his chest. The quiet eyes inched over my hand like a caterpillar, climbing the skin of my arm to my shoulder, neck, face. Eyes.

Eye contact. Something in me let go. I felt my heart fall backwards and land, surprised to look around and find that the tug-of-war was over, and Judah was safe, looking at me with his hopeful wordless eyes.

In that moment Judah gave me a great gift. I knew then something it takes most parents years to learn—that my child doesn't belong to me, he is himself, not a reflection of my ego. That he is not broken but whole—created in the image of God, a God who understands disability, because there are things even God can't control, things for which God needs our help.

Supper could wait. I took my son's hand. "Yes, Judah. I'll play trains with you," I said, and I turned off the stove.

Faith Paulsen *is a writer and a member of Gwynedd Friends Meeting in Gwynedd, Pennsylvania. This experience has been longing to be written for over 20 years.*

(*What Canst Thou Say?* June 2012 "Disabilities")

Out of the Blue

Carol Roth

As coordinator for seven meetings from 1989 to 1991, I visited each meeting often. I loved the long drive through many small towns, especially when the peach orchards were in full bloom. At home there were six children, and the constant calls for attention granted me scant time to breathe, let alone think, but on those long stretches of quiet country roads, I was able to enjoy my surroundings and savor the peace and quiet.

That's exactly what I was doing when I approached a portion of a heavily traveled road. It was favored by tractor-trailers, for once into the town it fed into other major routes. As usual, congestion was heavy on this road I had taken hundreds of times. Ahead lay a narrowed stretch of road caused by a small bridge over a creek. Crossing the bridge meant that one drove in a half-circle, which had been the scene of accidents. Coming toward me were three cars, followed by the high dome of a tractor-trailer. In back of me was a line of traffic.

I was focused on the road ahead when all of a sudden I heard words, *Look in your rearview mirror.* The words were sharp and loud as though being spoken by someone sitting beside me. My hands tightened on the steering wheel, my stomach gave a lurch, and as I was wondering where in the world these words were coming from I heard another command, *Do it now*! The words seemed to reverberate with an urgency I could not ignore.

My eyes flicked up to my rear-view mirror. I gasped out loud. In back of me, crossing over the solid white line, speeding up the road about four car lengths behind me, was a sporty red convertible. The three cars that had been coming toward me had gone by, but the driver in the convertible seemed oblivious to the tractor-trailer coming toward us fully in view, straightening out as it came around the curve. The driver of the red convertible was intent on passing all of us, and not only I but also everyone behind me was in for a massive chain reaction accident.

Other drivers blew their horns. What could I do to avoid this, to help stop this? I was about to reach closing distance with the semi when I heard the words, *Slow down.* Immediately, without hesitation, I began to slow down, praying the cars behind would see my brake lights. The red convertible was almost beside me. A young woman brushed her hair, one hand on the wheel. I braked harder, being careful not to come to a complete stop. I could hear the loud sound of the blaring horn from the tractor-trailer, the driver steering it to the right. I also steered my car to the right as far as I could.

The driver of the convertible never gave a hint that she saw either of us, that she understood the danger. She was beside me now. The opening created by the tractor-trailer driver and me was just wide enough for her to drive through, and she roared by without a backward glance as she sped around the half-curve; then she was out of sight. I was shaking but kept my car under control, easing back into the proper portion of my lane. I glanced at the tractor-trailer driver. His face was ashen. He tipped his hat and I nodded as we passed.

As I came fully to the end of the half-circle, I saw a police car, parked behind the red convertible. He must have been waiting to catch speeders. I pulled over and walked up to the police officer, who was bent over the driver's door. The young woman was screaming and cursing. I asked if I could speak to him about her and told him what she had done. All the while, she continued to curse, to demand she be allowed to go on her way. She then began to call me names, saying I was lying and she had not passed in a no-pass zone.

The police officer took statements from other drivers who also pulled over. When it became apparent she would not stop her raving, he locked her car up and placed her in the police car. I got in my own car and drove away, intending to go straight to the nearest meeting, but once I was back on country roads again, I knew I had to stop, to regroup, to regain some sense of peace. I stopped my car next to the first field I came to. It was covered in dense clover; yellow buttercups could be seen everywhere, and ahead was a cluster of trees. I sat under a large maple, grateful for the shade. I couldn't comprehend what I had experienced moments before.

Questions tumbled. Where had the warnings in my car come from? Without any notice, those three commands had come: *Look in your rearview mirror; Do it now; Slow down.* The words did not come as thoughts but as clear directives from someone present beside me. Something Holy had been in that car, granting me instantaneous foreknowledge of an event about to occur. I had been told what to do, when to do it, and my life had been spared as well as those of everyone around me. Tears welled as I realized just how real the danger had been and how those words had reached me just in time. My heart swelled with gratitude, awe, wonder, and thanksgiving at the soul-knowledge Someone cared about me and everyone else around me. Out of the blue, once again, communication with the Source; I whispered a fervent "Thank you" as I went on my way.

Carol Roth *is a poet, a writer, and a person on a journey to reach the center of her soul.*

(*What Canst Thou Say?* August 2004 "Knowings")

An Absolute Total Knowing

Jennifer Frick

When I entered Saint Mary's that morning in January of 1995, the church was empty and still. A few candles flickered in front of the statue of Mary. I had come to light a candle and to pray for my mother-in-law, Barb, during her surgery. I had just begun to pray when I was startled by an overwhelming sensation. It seemed to come from outside me. The feeling flooded through me, filled my chest and flowed down through my arms. I lived in constant doubt, but I could not explain or ignore it.

I opened my eyes and looked around. I stood up. I shook my arms and swung them about. I paced up and down the aisles of the church, but the feeling would not go away. It neither lessened nor changed, and did not fade until several hours after I left Saint Mary's.

There were no definite words, no voices ringing through the church or whispering in my ear. There was only this—absolute and total knowing: *She's not going to make it through this.* Yet, that she would die didn't seem likely. She'd had so many tests to see if she was strong enough for surgery. All of the doctors were certain she would be fine. And yet I knew. I knew as I had never known anything before.

I had told Barb just the night before that I had lit a candle and prayed for her, and that I would go back to the church and do the same the next day while she was in surgery. Although I was Quaker, my in-laws were Catholic, and I knew going to Saint Mary's and lighting a candle would mean something special to Barb.

She was scheduled to go into surgery at 8:30 Friday morning. A hundred little things caused me to run late, and I didn't get to church until a couple of hours later. I was so late I almost didn't go. I found out later she had gone into surgery late, and was still being operated on while I was praying for her.

I called my husband. She was fine. The doctors were pleased. *Should I say something? Should I tell him what happened in church?*

I decided to tell him, and we planned I would stay with my father-in-law. I didn't know what I could do; I just knew I didn't want him to be alone when his wife died. Monday passed uneventfully. The bypass surgery had worked; her toes were pink. What had the message meant?

Barb was a heavy smoker, and her lungs were not good. On Tuesday the doctors put in a breathing tube. It was very uncomfortable, and they sedated her.

She suffered a massive stroke. Half her brain was destroyed. On Friday, my father-in-law made the decision to turn off the machines. The doctors predicted she would last only a few hours, but her husband said, "She's a fighter," and he was right. She died Monday.

Why had I received this warning? David, my son, had died at birth a little over a year before, and I had received no such warning then. There were things I could have done to prevent David's death. It didn't seem fair. Why had I been warned about Barb but not David? It didn't make sense. I could do nothing for Barb, and yet I knew. But because I knew, I stayed with my father-in-law, and he was not alone.

I do not believe in predestination, and knowing something before it happens conflicts with my theology. And yet, in the end, there is only this: I knew.

Jennifer Frick *can't get clear to pray for anything else, or center, until she has prayed for others. She is a member of West Richmond Friends IN, and a graduate of Christian Theological Seminary.*

(*What Canst Thou Say?* August 2004 "Knowings")

A Vision of Sanity
Wendy Clarissa Geiger

Here is a vivid vision I experienced about 15-20 years ago while washing dishes at the kitchen sink. It's one of several signs that I might have a son some day, though I have chosen a celibate and childless life. A little background is in order. My parents, Julia and Alfred Geiger, met in the African American Freedom Struggle here in Jacksonville, Florida, thus thinking about racism was very much a part of my life. I used to ask my mother several times each year how she could have lived with such blatant racism when she was younger. "Didn't you just want to go out into the street and scream?" I'd ask. She'd answer, "People protested, and people got arrested."

In the vision, I see myself with a son doing the dishes together, This European American, blonde-haired, ten year-old son asks me, "Mama, what was it like to live with nuclear weapons? Didn't you just want to go out into the street and scream?" I answer him the same way my mother, in "real" life, answered me: "People protested, and people got arrested." That was the end of the vision and my return to an awareness of washing dishes at the kitchen sink.

When I'm despairing for the world and for its future, I remember this vision. And, the memory of this profound vision returns me to the task of ridding the world of nuclear weapons—viscerally aware that this will happen, is happening. Although, I am in the thick of the nuclear disarmament movement, mired in doubt and disappointment at times regarding the presence and proliferation of nuclear weapons, the memory of this vision gives me a glimpse of the big picture—when nuclear weapons will be no more—and my part in this struggle for justice, sanity, and peace. I am moved to think of our society as not suicidal, not genocidal, but omnicidal with the presence of nuclear weapons threatening all life on Earth. And, this vision at the kitchen sink gave me a glimpse of a time when society will actually be sane.

Wendy Clarissa Geiger *is a 48-year-old European American Quaker womun mystic, poet, writer and thinker, dwelling on the pine tree farm in Jacksonville, Florida, that's been in the Geiger family since 1898. Wendy joined Jacksonville Friends Meeting in 2012 and is co-clerk of Southeastern Yearly Meeting Worship and Ministry Committee.*

(*What Canst Thou Say?* February 2014 "Prophetic Vision")

With God in Pain and Despair

Therefore, to keep me from being too elated, a thorn was given to me in the flesh, a messenger of Satan to torment me, to keep me from being too elated. Three times I appealed to the Lord about this, that it would leave me, but he said to me, "My grace is sufficient for you, for power is made perfect in weakness." So, I will boast all the more gladly of my weaknesses, so that the power of Christ may dwell in me. Therefore I am content with weaknesses, insults, hardships, persecutions, and calamities for the sake of Christ; for whenever I am weak, then I am strong.
—2 Corinthians 12:7-10
(Contributed by Michael Hannah, May 2010 "Addiction")

Mystics, like all the rest of the human race, sometimes walk a treacherous path—homelessness, abuse, addiction, tragedy. But they also walk with a life Companion who gives courage.

Robin Arbiter writes of Sorrow as a life companion; Allison Randall, a natural contemplative, shares how she survives her shaming by singing hymns. Lee Rada makes hard choices as she walks through the Valley of Addiction to a happy life. Dalton Roberts wonders what Jesus wrote in the sand; and Carol Roth learns God knows our names as well as our souls.

Cathy Waisvisz's poem is inspired by Jesus' encounter with the man with demons. Alicia Adams almost rejects the one God sent to help, while Jacqueline Hannah dreams both her complicity and her redemption in God's compassionate gaze. Angeline Reeks sings of the shadows in her life and Michael Resman learns that mystical experiences lead to humility.

Anne Highland shares how choosing to breathe while remembering horrors leads to healing, and Lynn Kirby shares her gratitude in the face of horrors. Paul Schobernd in his near-death moment knows he is going home.

Our authors experience a blessed assurance that we really are never alone.

Promise and Pain

Robin Arbiter

Every woman is Jesus
when she's in love,
suspended on a cross
between promise and pain.

Monthly, she is bled
and held aloft,
her body pierced
to make a window
from which she can see
the whole of life,
or, if she chooses,
just the eyes
of those for whom
she climbed so high.

OhSorrow, Here You Are

Robin Arbiter

OhSorrow, here you are.
The days were crisp without you
And through the nights rode
 blood and moon.
There is one whose breath I
 breathed
And for whom I took you off
And draped you in my closet,
Plumshimmer barely visible.
Now I take you trimmed with
 silver
To cover me again.
The days are sluggish, the nights
 decay,
And I in my dullgarnet pain eat
 flesh in solitude,
Eschewing the leafy greens,
With only you Sorrow for comfort.

Lilith

Robin Arbiter

There she is
In unsteady flight
From an impending Christ.
She will fall:
She will fall and weep
For her too-small hands
And the imperfect path
Fading behind her.
She will, wounded,
Forget the site of her pain:
If only she could be loved!

Robin Arbiter is an artist, writer, and community activist living in Urbana, Illinois. The adopted daughter of Jewish parents who sent her to Christian Science Sunday Schools, she calls on the histories and traditions of many birth-and-choice ancestors in her work. She participates with Anne Scherer and Mariellen Gilpin in a twice-monthly writers' workshop exploring spiritually oriented writing.

(*What Canst Thou Say?* May 2013 "Meaning from Despair")

From Silence To Singing
Allison Randall

These things don't happen to nice girls. (I'm so ashamed.)
These things don't happen to good people. (I'm so ashamed.)
These things don't happen to people like me. (I'm so ashamed.)
These things don't happen in families like mine. (I'm so ashamed.)
People like my husband don't do things like this. (I'm so ashamed of him.)
What does it say about me that I married someone who would do this to me? (I'm so ashamed.)

All these things went through my head for many weeks after the sexual abuse, as I lay in my bed too frightened to sleep, as night after night I soaked in the tub in the middle of my broken sleep, trying to feel clean, as my mind perseverated, against my will, on the abuse.

How could I have allowed this to happen?

I felt as if "ABUSED!" were written on my forehead and everyone could tell by looking at me what had happened to me.

I gained 15 pounds in short order, disguising the body that had been shamed.

I wore shapeless clothes, hiding the body that had been shamed.

I wore grays and browns and tans, calling no attention to the body that had been shamed.

I hid from my friends and relatives, staying mostly to myself, embarrassed not only from the shame of the abuse itself, but also of all the strange symptoms of Post Traumatic Stress Disorder which had taken over my mind.

I was not myself.

I felt Alone. I was used to feeling the Presence of God, but much of the time now I felt as deserted by God as I did by my family and friends.

Shame was just a piece of what needed healing. There was also the pain in my heart from experiencing betrayal by the man I had been closest to, the resulting depression, fear. I was a wreck.

My longtime daily practice of meditation (transcendental type, clearing the mind for God) had become sometimes a time of not being able to get rid of all these thoughts, sometimes a time of just plain dryness. I have heard that when someone loses his sight, or hearing, the other senses are intensified, sharpened; when one way of communicating with the world is stopped, other ones develop. I have found something similar to be true of our communication with God. If our usual mode becomes nonfunctional, other ways present themselves, open up, blossom. Used to many years of daily spiritual practice, instead of abandoning that habitual time of waiting on the Lord, I tried substituting other spiritual practices. The mode that most helped me heal from shame was singing. A song that really spoke to me during that time was *Precious Lord*.

Precious Lord, take my hand,
Lead me on, help me stand,
I am weak, I am tired, I am worn.
Lead me on through the night
Lead me on to the Light,
Lead me on, precious Lord, take my hand.

All that was good. A sung prayer. But one line in particular, from the second verse, was especially helpful:

When the way be drear, Precious Lord, linger near.

Even when I couldn't feel the presence of God, I imagined It lingering near, just out of reach. All I had to do was, as in yoga, practice stretching, stretch a little more, reach out, not give up.

I knew all along at the intellectual level that the shame didn't really belong to me, but to my then husband. But somehow in our society the shame of abuse still falls upon the women, and we keep accepting it because intimate violation seems so shameful. When we are shamed, we need someone to hold our hand, to stand up for us, to speak for us, and yes, to tell us we will eventually be Whole. Abuse is something most human beings want to distance themselves from, either because they are embarrassed by it or have no idea how to deal with the now unrecognizable person in front of them.

My healing came slowly, over many years, and still continues. I didn't give up on God and God didn't give up on me. I stretched, God lingered near, held my hand, and so did some friends. We all got closer, re-entered each others' hearts. Grace happens. Healing happens. A very large Love holds us all.

Allison Randall *is a member of Keene Worship Group (New Hampshire). She says that since that time she has lost much of the weight, and regularly wears all sorts of bright colors. She attempts to be aware as much as possible of the ways God might be working in her life, and to be grateful.*

(*What Canst Thou Say?* February 2012 "Shame")

From Addiction to Happiness
Lee Rada

I met a wonderful man. He was warm, funny, smart and ever so talented. He wasn't a knight in shining armor, but I was sure he held my ticket to happiness. We shared common interests and, even more important, he seemed to want to spend time with me.

After a few months I found out there was one little problem—he admitted he sometimes took a day or two off to smoke cocaine. That explained the longer-than-expected absences when I thought I had gotten some of his travel dates wrong.

Still, love conquers all, right? All I had to do was fix him and then we could live happily ever after. I came up with all sorts of diversions to keep him busy and in my company. I spent many evenings and weekends with him. When we couldn't be together, he promised he would call me if he felt like using. If he called me late at night, I would keep him on the phone until he fell asleep. One month I insisted that I should be in charge of his money; I bought his groceries, paid his bills and gave him a small allowance.

Still, despite my best efforts, he would go out and use anyway. Each time this happened, I was devastated. How had I failed as a friend? Or more to the point, how could he pick crack over me? My life began to revolve around his binges. I would count his days clean. I figured out a way to monitor his drug use by checking his bank balance by phone. Sometimes I would call the automated teller system every fifteen minutes. A withdrawal meant he was still alive, but still using. When there was no activity for a while, I convinced myself he had overdosed and was probably dead. I was happiest when there was no more money in the account, because that meant he would be home soon.

Every binge would be his last. Except when it wasn't. There were more and more difficult situations. Stranded in a city miles away? Of course I would send bus fare. Going to rehab this month? I could pay the rent. How did that verse go? *I was hungry and you fed me, I was in prison and you visited me.* I did that, too. I followed the rules, but my prayers were pretty much being ignored. Maybe there was another way. I decided to look online.

I found the Co-Anon E meeting. At first I didn't like what these program people had to tell me. They had no cures for addiction; they didn't even have any helpful hints. They said I should focus on my recovery, yet I was the person who didn't have a drug problem. My only problem was getting my loved one to stop doing drugs. Or was it?

"Let go and let God," they told me. I wasn't so sure. Then again, my way hadn't gone too well. Picking up his expenses had put me in debt. Emotionally I was a wreck. I was increasingly resentful, fearful, depressed and confused, as I allowed my life to become more consumed by the darkness of drug use—yet I didn't even get high. The longtime members had a sense of peace and serenity that I wanted. Finally I decided to try it their way. I had little to lose.

One of my new online friends encouraged me to do a Fourth Step workshop with her, including the dreaded Fearless Moral Inventory. I was afraid I would finally be exposed as the defective, horrible person I tried so carefully to hide from the world—and summarily rejected by my sponsor and my new friend. Still, I followed the process. I looked at my anger, my fears, my shortcomings. I faced myself. And I faced God. To my great surprise it was a very self-affirming and liberating experience.

I decided what I wanted to keep—and what I wanted to give up. Doing things my way hadn't always worked out so well, so surrendering to the creator of the universe didn't seem like such a bad proposition. If there really was such a thing as sin, trying to control people and outcomes might be on the list—especially when the manipulation was masked behind seemingly kind and selfless actions. On a more practical level, trying to be responsible for another person's actions and happiness was exhausting.

Almost immediately I came to believe that I was really no better—and no worse—than anyone else. I began to release many of my issues about not being good enough, as I surrendered my defects to the universe. I realized the creator of the universe wasn't judging me, so why was I living in fear of what another person's opinions might be? When I finally accepted that my friend's life was between him and God, just as mine was, I found a great deal of peace. I was able to release him and actually become grateful for the experience, because it brought me so much closer to the Truth.

I found myself returning to activities and friends I had given up in the years when I had allowed my focus to become skewed. Some years before, I had done meditation work, which involved creating sacred space within and without and moving energy through my chakras. I came back to those practices with new zeal and far deeper understanding.

Some of the change came with time, and many things remain to be changed. Sometimes I can be self-righteous or take a "poor me" victim attitude. Sometimes I worry about what other people think, or try to run things my way. Sometimes I am just self-righteous and intolerant.

Through the internet I also found a nearby Quaker meeting. Attending Meeting for Worship helps me center down and attend to the still small voice of the Universe. And when I am in tune with the Universe, which is my term for the Higher Power referenced in the 12 Steps, I have found things have a way of working out perfectly well. I have found that deep sense of inner peace…and, most curiously, happiness.

Lee Rada *attends Morningside Meeting, New York City. She is relatively new to Quakerism, but she was a Quaker a long time before she knew it. Through a West African dance instructor she has discovered spiritual renewal through movement. She is working on a book about her life.*

(*What Canst Thou Say?* May 2010 "Addiction and Grace")

I Wonder What He Wrote In The Sand

Dalton Roberts

*She was just a woman of the street;
They threw her in shame at Jesus' feet.
As they stood there with stones in their hands
He stooped and wrote something in the sand.*

*I think He wrote, "You can always start again;
No matter who you are or what you've been,
I'll help you if you'll give me your hand."
I wonder what He wrote in the sand.*

*They said, "Master, she should die for her wrong."
He said, "If you have no sin, then cast your stone."
One by one they dropped them from their hands
At the words He was writing in the sand.*

*I think He wrote, "Only love can change a man.
So love one another, it's the great command."
As He stood there with her life in His hand
I wonder what he wrote in the sand.*

Happy Doghouse Music (BMI). Reprinted with the author's permission.

(*What Canst Say?* February 2012 "Shame")

Our Names Are Known

Carol Roth

In the summer of 1972 there came an opportunity that my husband Frank felt he couldn't pass up. He had been offered employment on a missile base site on the atoll of Kwajalein in the South Pacific. He would leave immediately and then send for me and our five-year-old daughter Susan to join him. This change would also give us a break in our stormy marriage. Frank was a deeply troubled man, given to bouts of physical abuse. I had sought help from his beatings from clergy, from the police. There were no support groups available, and shelters for abused women were non-existent. I had learned to become a silent victim, to pretend all was well. Now, it seemed as though there was a possibility that everything could really change for us. I watched him board his plane, his face happy, hopeful.

All of a sudden, this formerly cold, always angry man was sending warm, loving tapes home. He spoke of the beauty of the South Pacific, of the housing he was securing for us, of how much he missed us. I obeyed his orders to sell everything we owned to fly out to join him.

It turned out to be the worst decision I ever made. Frank was there when our plane landed. His face was dark and angry as he led us to another plane that would take us five hundred miles to a tiny atoll called Majuro. At the last moment housing for Susan and me on Kwajalein had fallen through. We would have to stay on Majuro while he flew in once every thirty days to check on us. It was going to cost him extra money and he was livid at the cost.

Frank hardly looked at his child. When our plane landed at Majuro he took us to a run-down crowded house filled with feces and filth, swarming with flies. For the next three months Susan and I lived in a tiny room, existing mostly on tuna covered with so many roaches it looked as if it was moving; gray, moldy bread and bloody chicken. Frank did fly in once a month, forcing me to have sex with him. He berated me for losing weight and for Susie and me always being ill.

We escaped because a kind Marshallese neighbor contacted a visiting doctor who was making tours of the atolls. Frank was warned back on Kwajalein to send us back to the States. Furious, he complied and provided airfare for Susan and me. We staggered off the plane into the waiting arms of relatives. Susan was covered with lice and open sores. I weighed seventy pounds. But we were alive, we were together, and he could not hurt us anymore.

My sister and her husband moved us into their home. The first few weeks passed in an exhausted haze. Susan had a fever that would not come down. I did call an attorney and told him I wanted to file for divorce. Meanwhile, my sister took my daughter to her family doctor, who stated Susan would need extensive and expensive tests to determine what kind of parasites had infected her. We had no medical insurance card. I had no money, no job, and was in no condition to search for one. My sister and her husband could not afford to have my daughter treated. My sister told me we could still have Frank pay for the tests. Though we were separated, he was legally responsible for her care until we were divorced. I was stunned when she further told me that Frank had quit his job, flown home and was now living in a neighboring state. He had called to tell her that he was sorry that everything had gone so wrong.

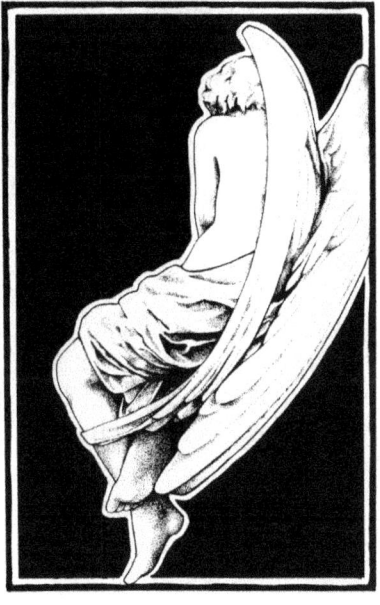

Ink drawing by Marcella Beaty who writes, "In my experience, angels aren't always beaming with radiance; they have been quiet, basically mute, yet solid...like stone...like statuary"

Sick in body, broken in spirit, I called him. I pleaded with him to send me the medical card I needed to have tests done for Susan. He stipulated if I wanted the card, I would have to meet him where he lived. My sister was giving Susan a bath when I slipped out of the house and took a bus to meet with Frank. Once in the city I boarded the El and finally arrived at the meeting place. I saw him waiting in his car and moved slowly toward it, praying, praying that he would just give me the card and let me leave in peace.

My stomach and face hurt from the blows that Frank delivered the second I entered the car. My head reeled from the filthy words he screamed at me. Empty-handed and without the card I needed for Susan, I had yanked open the door and lurched down the steaming hot, dirty, deserted city street. From behind, I heard the screech of his tires as he sped away.

I moved closer to the brick wall of an abandoned factory building, its windows and doors boarded up. The sky overhead had suddenly darkened with threatening storm clouds.

I began to shiver. I felt so alone. There had been times of such hunger and fatigue on the island, yet I had always felt God was with me and that Susan and I would survive. But now, all I could feel was emptiness. I didn't know what to do. How was I going to provide for my daughter, support her and myself? Oh, God, I was so tired. Was there no way to end this cycle of darkness, no way to escape all this pain?

From inside of me there came a thought so sharp and loud that I had to stop walking. My husband had life insurance policies on my daughter and me. I had already begun proceedings for the divorce and I had custody of our daughter. I wasn't certain, but the fact we were divorcing could mean that if I died, my life insurance money would go to my daughter. Frank's treatment of us, especially the condition that Susan and I were in after our stay on Majuro, would prove his neglect and cruelty. Surely, he would never be granted custody of her. With my life insurance money my sister could afford to give Susan everything she needed. Yes, this was the way out. My death would secure the lifestyle Susan deserved.

I began to hurry, staggering as I went. The El platform was ahead. I would jump from the platform onto the tracks. It was nearing rush hour, the trains would be packed with people, and no one would notice me.

"*Carol.*" What was that? Where was that voice coming from? I tried to move faster through the thick, humid air. I had to do this before I lost my nerve.

"*Carol.*" I turned and saw a man keeping pace with my steps. He looked like a common, everyday worker dressed in a green plaid shirt and light brown chinos. He was looking right at me. His facial features were fine but not delicate. He had an aquiline nose and a strong chin. His hair was medium length and soft brown. His eyes startled me. They were so beautiful, dark brown and so clear, filled with compassion. I felt strange and trembled inside. No one had ever looked at me this way. I could feel warmth flowing from him toward me.

"How do you know my name?" I stammered. What did he want? Where did he come from? He had appeared out of nowhere. Whoever he was, he was keeping me from concentrating on what I had to do. I had no time for this.

"*Oh, we know your name. We know what you are intending to do. We know about Susan also.*"

Absolute shock coursed through my body. I stopped my onward thrust toward the El. I faced him and cried out, "How do you know her name? How do you know my daughter's name?"

"*We know everything.*" he replied. "*Don't do it, Carol. Don't do it.*"

I shrank back from him. My heart was pounding, pounding. I began to walk again, trying to get away from him. Angrily, I cried, "I have to do this! You don't understand! I am not a good mother. I can't give Susan anything she needs. Leave me alone. I have to do this!"

Intimacy with God in Times of Pain and Despair

"No, you do not. Susan has everything that she needs in the love you feel for her. The two of you will be fine."

Oh, his voice. It covered me, spreading warmth and love through me. He continued to speak, each word deliberate, steady. *"Your life is important, Carol. Each life has great purpose and meaning. There is work ahead for you to do. Don't do this. Go home to Susan. She's waiting for you."*

Shame filled me. I looked away from him. I could not bear to look into his eyes, so filled with a beautiful inner light. Total love and acceptance came from this stranger. Oh, God, what had I been thinking of! I turned to tell him I had changed my mind. I would go back to my daughter and do my best to give her the life she deserved.

He was gone! He had not passed by me. How had he left so quickly? The air was suddenly still and it had changed. It felt cleaner, sweeter, and I could breathe easier. I reached the El station. I purchased my token and joined the other people ready to board the train. I felt as though I were moving in a cocoon of peace, protected from all harm.

As I settled into my seat on the train, I stared down at the street. Only moments before the stranger appeared, it had seemed to be so ugly, dark, and cold. But now the sun was streaming and the streets bustled with people moving about in the Light. With renewed strength and determination, I rode the train back to the daughter that I had almost left behind.

I write this so others can know that we are loved with a Love that has no limits, that knows all of our faults and accepts us just as we are. As you stagger in the darkness, as you search for meaning in a life that seems cold and empty, know this: you are never alone. There is one who walks alongside of you, who is waiting to speak with you. Believe this: Our Names Are Known.

Carol Roth formerly served on the WCTS editorial team and resigned due to chronic health problems. She wrote this story in between doctor appointments and plans for further surgeries.

(*What Canst Thou Say?* November 2008 "Angels")

Legion's Healing*

Cathy Waisvisz

Black corroded shards of death
rip my heart, infect my soul
Tormented I tear off my clothes
my chains
everything my chains
Receiving abandonment
I seek shelter with the dead
my eyes and skin feasting on their rest
the cool tombstones as balm
welcome oasis to my senses
Still my last chance dark horse
plunges on
to crash and burn with me on it
I tell you this with only screams
You seem to already know
Naked and raw and unwittingly
I communicate without words
You are not afraid of catching madness
You do not run in fear as others do
Somehow your presence calms me
I want to linger here
Cool catacombs are waiting
shying horse with blinders on
confusion wakes a choice to make
escape or test this balm
You reach out and touch me
a spark in my body slowly spreads
infused with heat I fear torture
your presence commands I remain
I boil, then simmer, then cool
relief sweeps over my brow
The catacombs can wait
I am not abandoned now
I notice I have clothes on
how or when was lost in the haze
buzzing crowds' clothes keep them warm
my warmth comes from your love

Cathy Waisvisz did not "take" well to formal education and was more concerned about what was going on out the window or had her nose in a novel, and with self-education came freedom and exploration of world history, psychology and the arts. Her employment has included work at the University of Illinois Foundation but since her marriage two years ago she has taken advantage of writing workshops and singing with the Parkland Chorus, and came to the Quaker Friends' Meeting in Urbana after her former Lutheran church disbanded; she likes the Quakers also because she is free.

(*What Canst Thou Say?* May 2013 "Meaning from Despair")

*Biblical reference: Luke 8:27, 29-31
27 *As he stepped ashore he was met by a man from the town who was possessed by devils. ...*
29 *For Jesus was already ordering the unclean spirit to come out of the man. Many a time it had seized him, and then, for safety's sake, they would secure him with chains and fetters; but each time he broke loose, and with the devil in charge, made off to the solitary places.*
30 *Jesus asked him, "What is your name?"*
"Legion," he replied.
31 *This was because so many devils had taken possession of him. And they begged him not to banish them to the Abyss.*

Intimacy with God in Times of Pain and Despair ◄ 111

The One Sent to Help

Alicia Adams

I was homeless and ill. Following my guidance, I found myself in a park in Wickenburg, Arizona. "Now what?" I asked my spiritual Teachers, who were guiding me step by step.

"Wait!" they told me. "We are sending someone to meet you. Perhaps they will offer their assistance."

It was getting dark and cold. I felt very alone as I waited in the deserted park. I was also getting frightened. I sensed that someone was watching me. I caught glimpses of him as he moved between the bushes, his attention focused on me. I packed up my notebook, which I used to communicate with my Teachers, and prepared to move to the other side of the park. He stumbled into the open, headed for me.

He was old and shabbily dressed and, as he approached, I noted that he was none too clean. He staggered a bit. "A drunk," I thought. No one to fear but also no one I wished to be with! I got quickly to my feet and picked up my pack.

"All alone, Dearie?" he asked me.

"No, I'm just waiting for friends to pick me up," I replied.

"I didn't mean to frighten you, Dearie," he continued. "I thought that if you were all alone, you might like to come home with me."

That was the last thing I wanted to do! I thanked him politely but said my friends would be here soon. He staggered off. Relieved, I sat down again and pulled out my notebook. "What now?" I wrote. "It's getting dark and cold. I can't stay here."

"You refused his help."

"Who?" I wrote. "I didn't talk to anybody—except that old drunk!"

"That old drunk, as you call him, is the one sent to help you."

I was stunned. "What do you mean? I can't go with him! Why would you send him to me?"

"God doesn't see him as you do," was the reply. *"God sees his heart. He wanted to help you. He knows all about being lonely."*

I was shown, then, that God sees our love—not our outer appearances. Of all the people in the town, this man was the only one to offer to share what he had with me. I was broken down in my pride; I was ashamed. When he returned, to repeat his invitation, I went home with him. I slept on a couch on the front porch of his very small trailer. It was very dirty—strewn with his clothes and dirty dishes. At one point, I tried to clean for him. "I don't need you for cleaning!" he corrected me. "I need you for company!" Thus I learned that a drunk may be an angel, the one sent to help.

Alicia Adams *is a member of Berkeley Meeting, California.*

(*What Canst Thou Say?* November 2008 "Angels")

Angel in a Trench Coat

Jacqueline Z. W. Hannah

Monday, April 28, 2008, 5:59 a.m.

I dreamed last night of innocence. *A police detective in a long coat has come to question me as a witness. It becomes clear he knows a lot about me. I share some small thing about my life to give context to what I am saying to him and he already knows this small, personal thing. I suppose I should notice and start to be worried, but I am not, at least not yet. Then I bring up the murder.*

I am living in a very large home that is shared by five or six people as I was in '94. But in the dream, unlike reality, a woman has been murdered in that house during the time I was living there. When I bring up the murder I am very calm at first, very matter-of-fact about it, just a side note brought up as part of another point. But the detective's response, "Yeah, we are still looking for a left-handed person connected to that," sent chills down my spine. I am left-handed.

Is this what this officer is really here about? Is he here to trick me? Does he think I am the missing murderer? The conversation goes on as if he never mentioned it, as if it is just a conversational aside too unrelated to our topic to even comment on, but I strongly suspect it was done on purpose, to get a rise out of me. I feel guilty, horribly guilty. Was I involved? Had I been an accomplice?

I am afraid I was an accomplice of some kind. My conscience feels bloodstained and shamed, but I do not know why. I have no clear memory of ever doing anything that day, though I was in the house when it happened. I have only my conscience to go by, and it feels filthy. The conversation with the detective continues as I search inside myself. The detective moves on to interview another potential witness who is waiting in the next room.

I notice that we are in my grandmother's house, full of good memories for me and yet the constant ghost of knowing. These walls contain the history of all the rage and abuse my grandfather showered on my grandmother, my mother, my aunts and uncles. And I begin to feel suspicious of myself. I look back at my life and it isn't just this murder, for I have been close to many crimes and acts of violence. Perhaps I am pretending to be an innocent bystander to all of these events, but beneath my hazy denials I am actually part of the violence in each one. Perhaps I am guilty, guilty, guilty.

I go after the detective and ask if I can speak to him again. "If, hypothetically, someone were to share information about someone else that might have been involved in a crime, would, oh, never mind . . ." Why am I asking this? I don't know, but I suspect myself of being about to share some false testimony to send the cop off in some other direction to make myself look innocent of being the bad, bad person I am.

As I am talking to the cop, I realize two things. One, I am naked from the waist up. Two, I really am scared of turning over some knowledge that might help in that old murder case. There is something buried in that haze of memory that is coming to the surface and I am trembling with it. I think, "Why even tell him? He must think I am a horrible criminal because he knows enough about me to know I was nearby or a witness to all those crimes. He won't believe me."

But I do tell him, words just come as I wrap my arms around myself and shake. "I wasn't the only left-handed person in that house," I say quietly, staring at the wall next to his head. "I was in the house. I did hear something. There was this man; I don't think I ever knew his name.

"I should have called the cops, but I didn't know back then you could call 911 about something like that. That I could just say, 'Hey, I heard this short female scream and then this thump on the floor above me and I don't know that anything bad happened but I have a bad feeling,' I thought I'd get in trouble for making a non-emergency call to 911, that they would just tell me to go check it myself."

I look up at the detective, wanting something but not knowing what, too far gone now to try to protect myself from how exposed I am physically and emotionally. His eyes are not hard, I even sense some kindness in them— had it been there all along? Is it my own expectation that he is looking to find me guilty that has made me think he is trying to trick me into confessing to something?

His exact words escape me now, but he tells me that he knows about the other left-handed person in the house, that he knows it is a man, that he has a vague description of him but nothing else and that he has never suspected me. His words are gentle, and with his gentleness it comes to me that I really am innocent. I have not done anything wrong, I was never a part of a murder or any of those other things I witnessed just because I was not able to prevent them or to do something about it afterwards. In none of those circumstances *was I in a position to do anything; if I had done anything I was likely to have gotten hurt myself at worst, disbelieved and ignored at best.*

There is a sense of lightness since I woke up from that dream. The cliché is true, "I feel as if a great weight has been lifted from me." Not from my shoulders, but from my chest and stomach. I feel as if my lungs are opening more deeply, more easily, are taking in so much more oxygen with so much less effort than before. I feel wrapped in great and gentle arms, like a child that has found solace in a parent's embrace and is believed, cherished.

"What was that dream all about?" I ask myself. I suppose I don't really need to know, but as I ask myself, things float to the surface. Times that I was in the house when a friend's parents were drunk and slapped her so hard that blood was coming from her mouth. Times when a friend's parents said horrible, shaming, untrue things to her in front of all of us at her birthday party and I wanted to kill them. I never knew I felt so guilty about it, that I had felt such shame for not protecting them all or speaking up for them—until now, when the responsibility has been lifted from my shoulders by Spirit dressed in a detective's trench coat. I still want to be able to go back and stop those things from happening, but I no longer feel shame. I just feel like having a good cry.

Jacqueline Z. W. Hannah *is a member of Urbana-Champaign meeting, Illinois. She has a calling to bring whole foods, not produced by slave labor, to the community through the Common Ground food coop.*

(*What Canst Thou Say?* November 2008 "Angels")

Shadows

Angeline Reeks

*Shadows in my mind
are hopes and dreams and fears.
No substance to them now,
and yet, when someone nears
enough to breach the inner space,*

*They spring to life, full-blown,
and live, and die, and once again
become, just shadows in my mind.*

Angeline Reeks is a member of Upper Fox Valley Meeting, Illinois, and a member of Ministry and Advancement Committee, Illinois Yearly Meeting.

(*What Canst Thou Say?* May 2010 "Addiction and Grace")

Intimacy with God in Times of Pain and Despair

Hard Lessons

Michael Resman

Some may believe that to step onto the spiritual path results in contemplating meadows of wild flowers and butterflies under a gentle sun. One's spiritual journey may produce bliss. But spirituality is not for the faint-hearted, for lessons can also be learned from the depths of despair.

Early in my journey I was shown the glory of God, followed by a clear vision of my own flaws and limitations. The contrast was raw and deep. After several weeks of these contrasting visions I was in such pain from seeing my own imperfections that I prayed aloud—something I never did. I pleaded with God to lift my pain, because I couldn't take any more.

Immediately, the burden was lifted from my heart and I was comforted. The agony I had known when shown my limitations was powerful enough to teach me a life lesson. It might be tempting to think that having mystical experiences makes me special, but I know better. I need to walk in humility.

Mike Resman recently retired because he felt called to a new career—praying. He spends hours each day in prayer activities: silent prayer, walking in parks, and cross stitching children's clothing for a homeless shelter. In order to leave adequate time for prayer, he has avoided taking on other tasks. He continues to follow a long-term call to write. He is Clerk of Rochester, Minnesota, Friends Meeting.

(*What Canst Thou Say?* May 2013 "Meaning from Despair")

The Next Breath

Anne C. Highland

"Just take one day at a time," my friends told me when I confided how intense my emotional pain was. Clearly, they had never felt pain like this, because one day of it was far beyond bearing. And this pain in my inner life was lasting for months, in strange contrast to my outer life, at home and at work, which was going well.

"Sounds like a dark night of the soul," said Sr. Mary, as she loosened my knotted muscles on the massage table. "Have you ever read St John of the Cross?"

"No," I said. I did not add that my brief foray into St. Augustine in college had ended any desire to read medieval theologians.

"We have it in the Convent library. I'll get it for you after our session," she said.

At home, opening the frayed volume of the *Dark Night of the Soul*, I felt as if a friend had joined me in my living room, one who had walked a path that felt like mine. With his words, my path was not so lonely.

As he said, it was a time of testing, a time of pruning, a time when we outgrew who we had been and were giving birth to the next phase of our lives. But how was I going to survive being tested, being pruned, when it meant enduring day after day of such intense pain? I felt myself becoming worn down by the burden of maintaining my outer life when nothing external seemed capable of cutting through my inner pain. I refused to consider medicating the pain away.

A year went by in this way, and then another. One day I simply reached my breaking point. Aloud, I said to the Universe, "That's it. I've done more inner work than anyone I know, and if this is what I get, then I quit. From now on, I am going to live in my anger at life! I know that living in that bitterness will probably bring back my cancer, and that's okay. I've had enough."

Instantly I heard a sweet inner voice say, urgently, "Oh, don't! You have come so far!" I was floored. My inner guidance generally informed me with subtle nudgings—a word, an image, a connection. Rarely had I heard clear sentences. But I was shocked into staying on the path of seeking growth and enlightenment.

I had to find a way to survive. One day at a time was too long. One hour at a time, one minute at a time were too much. As the days of pain went on, I fell further down, fearing that this well was bottomless. But the day came when I found the bottom and it felt like a stone floor. I had reached the maximum emotional pain I could endure, and I was still alive, still functioning. Standing on that stone floor, I owned the courage to breathe into the next moment of pain—to live one breath at a time.

Paradoxically, I began to appreciate the gifts of being present with the breath without expectation. And then, as spring sun warms the frozen earth, new life began to flow through me.

Anne C. Highland *is a clinical psychologist in private practice in Philadelphia. She attends Gwynedd Meeting. She is writing a book from her experiences.*

(*What Canst Thou Say?* November 2004 "Darkness")

Intimacy with God in Times of Pain and Despair

Gratitude in the Face of ....

Lynn Kirby

Even life's darkest situations bring blessings. Gratitude is possible in the midst of our grief and fears.

Schizophrenia struck our daughter when she was twenty-five, and she has been hospitalized at least a dozen times in the twenty intervening years. Serious psychotic episodes have been interspersed with periods of relative sanity, but she has never fully escaped from delusions and hallucinations. Unable to work, she has lived below the poverty line and has sometimes believed her family and friends were The Enemy. Her life has been hard, and yet she has deep love for God and a sense of being His.

It took years of despair for me to accept that my golden child had this cruel and undeserved illness, permanently. Along the way, I had a vision in which God reassured me that I would be shown how to live in peace and trust instead of anger and fear. I began to see that no matter what happens, even when scary and dangerous, the results will not be all bad. God will take care of us and give us what we need, always, even against our wishes.

I am deeply grateful for the gift of trust. What is best doesn't depend on my decisions, desires, and actions; a far wiser One will take care of it all. I have come to understand that solutions beyond my imagination will come in time. I don't even have to understand what comes—I only need to be open to receive guidance. What a relief to know that I am not in charge!

I am also grateful for another lesson I have learned, a surprising one. Society marginalizes, ignores, or persecutes people with mental illness. Underneath her personal reality, my daughter has a kind, tender, generous heart. She has taught me that one's personality and surface appearance can hide depths of love; that inside each of us is one of God's cherished children. From this, I am learning to let go of judgment of others.

She has no husband or children, and I have sometimes worried about her dying alone and uncared for. But she is dying now. Amidst the sadness I feel, I can still be very grateful that she is not alone, and that her father and I can give her support and love now. I thank God for giving us the health and strength she needs. Above all, I am grateful for the gift of this person who has so profoundly touched my life in more ways than I can possibly count.

Lynn Kirby *is a member of the Stevens Point, Wisconsin, Friends Meeting.*

(*What Canst Thou Say?* February 2009 "Gratefulnes")

Intimacy with God

I'll Bring My Own Rocks
Paul Schobernd

It was a Sunday in October, 1967. It was raining, and I had gone to my place of employment, because I was looking for the guy who had poisoned our coffee. He had put a can of Prince Albert tobacco in our coffee. My cousin and I had spent the night vomiting and shaking. I meant to do him physical harm. I was sixteen. But he was gone—drafted to go to Viet Nam—so he knew he was safe.

I was on my way back home when I hit a patch of mud. Being an inexperienced driver, I over-steered the car, and an oncoming car ran half through my car as I slid sideways. There was a family of five in the car, and the mother was killed instantly. It was half an hour before they managed to get me out.

Our first stop was at the funeral home. This was in rural Calhoun County, Illinois, where most of the entries to the county were by river ferry, and there was one bridge in Hardin, Illinois. We were closer to the bridge, and in that time the undertaker was also the ambulance service. My future wife's father was driving the ambulance, and I remember telling him I loved his daughter and intended to marry her. I wanted to make sure I said that, in case I died. It was two hours before I got to the hospital in Alton, Illinois, forty miles away.

We got to the hospital, where I was immediately placed in the intensive care unit. Intensive Care was a ward with six beds down each side and striped curtains separating the beds. I was in a coma, and it was probably about the third day that I had an out-of-body experience. I was going down a tunnel toward the light. I felt so good; I never felt so good. I was warm all over. I felt like I was going home. There were people waiting for me. All I could tell was that the people were my family. It was during this time that the doctor told my parents that I probably would not live through the night, and if I did, I would be paralyzed permanently.

Before I could reach that light, a voice that I assumed to be God said to me, "You must go back. It's not your time." And it was at that time that I came back to my body and discovered I was lying in glass. My kidneys had failed, but I knew that I was not going to die. I was unconscious, but God had spoken and I knew I was not going to die. But I couldn't communicate that to my parents, who were crying. It was the first time I'd ever seen my father cry. Somewhere along in this time—it's hard to tell when something begins and ends in a coma—I became aware of a woman screaming and yelling at the top of her lungs. Once again, I really wanted to do her harm. I was not a terribly enlightened person.

Intimacy with God in Times of Pain and Despair

This is where God turns evil to good. Out of my body, I went down around the striped curtain and looked the woman in the face. And I was immediately melted down and overcome with love and empathy. Mary was her name, and her gallbladder operation had not gone well. She was in tremendous pain, and there was nothing much they could do for her. I went back to my body, and I'm looking at myself. I re-entered my body content in knowing that God would not let me die, and I would in fact walk again. I think the lesson in seeing Mary and experiencing that unconditional love for someone I didn't know helped me to understand that God was with me. And I had that same unconditional love applied to me.

Shortly thereafter I woke from the coma. It wasn't until I left the ICU that I started to be scared that I would not walk. I started to forget the miracle that I'd seen and experienced. I was a very conservative Lutheran, and I had no religious construct on which to hang the ICU experience. And then I relapsed into my old ways of bartering with God for my life. A minister came to see me, and in private I told him the story of what had happened in the ICU. The man turned white. He read me scriptures and said prayers to protect me from evil. And he left as fast as he could. Thus I learned not to tell anyone about what had happened.

And, except for my wife, I told no one about my experience for fifteen more years. I was afraid of being ridiculed, and I was afraid also because I still did not understand what had occurred.

It wasn't until I read Moody's books on near-death experiences and found new ways of experiencing God that I learned not to fear what I didn't understand. And I learned to become more expansive in my acceptance of myself and others. I resigned my job as trustee in the Lutheran church. Shortly thereafter we wrote the church a check for the remainder of our tithe and left for good.

We found our Quaker home at Friends Hill in Quincy, Illinois, where it still took me some time to clear my mind. Iris Bell was probably the most important catalyst as I moved from being a scared wounded Lutheran to a new theology of expansiveness, acceptance, love, forgiveness—both for myself and others. I think the final event that really closed that chapter was when I sat in the swing at Friends Hill with my wife and pondered the need for water baptism. I couldn't let go of it. But as we were swinging, it started to rain, and every time we swung out we got wet. And a voice in my head very clearly said, "So you want water baptism. Here it is." That seemed to be the final issue.

I never blanked the out-of-body experience out of my memory banks. I kept thinking about it over the years. I developed ulcers, thinking about that family growing up without a mother, until I was finally able to forgive myself. Today I still say a prayer for that family, but not out of guilt anymore. I think the experience in the early days made me foolhardy, because I didn't fear death anymore. I lived on the edge, because I knew that the worst that could happen was that you would die, and since I'd already been there once I wasn't afraid of going back.

Today I experience life and the afterlife as separated by a very thin veil. In deep meditation we can touch that boundary and both give and receive feelings, messages and support without fear, knowing that energy is not destroyed but simply changes form. We are all part of the same entity.

As John Woolman said in his dream, he could no longer experience himself as a separate being. I think this metaphor is very much supported by quantum theory, and we can take the fear and mystery out of experiencing life and death. We distinguish ourselves by name for the sake of convenience. But at our essence, we are all One.

My granddaughter and I had a discussion after her aunt had lost twin babies. I said I thought probably they had gone to heaven. And she said,

"Yes, they have, and you know what?"

"What?" I said.

"Animals go to heaven too," she said.

"Even spiders?" I asked.

"My daddy doesn't like spiders," she said.

"How about worms?" I asked.

"I don't like worms," she said.

"But they're all animals," I said.

And she allowed that worms and spiders could go to heaven, too.

"What about trees?" I asked.

"I don't think so," she said.

"But trees are born, and they live and they die. They just don't move much," I said.

She allowed trees could go to heaven. We had already allowed water in heaven, since fish needed water, and they were animals.

"How about rocks?" I asked.

"No," she said.

I didn't argue with her beyond that, but we know that rocks are mostly space between the molecules, just as we are, so I suspect we might find rocks in heaven.

Intimacy with God in Times of Pain and Despair

It dawned on me after we'd finished our conversation that what we were really talking about was a version of heaven that described a perfect earth. It wasn't the theology of angels and clouds, harps and endless hymn singing for eternity. And this version of heaven sounded much more palatable than the one we're often given, even though it is considered a heresy by the Catholic Church.

It seems to me that if you want to know the unvarnished truth, you ask a five year old. And in this case, I'd rather go to her heaven, and I'll bring my own rocks.

In the final analysis we never stop learning, and stopping to learn from the least of God's creatures is where we are more apt to see the truth with a capital T.

Paul Schobernd *was Illinois Yearly Meeting's first Field Secretary, and a spiritual mentor to many. He was a member of Clear Creek Meeting, McNabb, Illinois. A few months before he died, editor Mariellen Gilpin showed up on his doorstep, laptop in hand, and typed this story while he dictated. She read it at his memorial, and was invited to submit it to* Among Friends, *the Illinois Yearly Meeting newsletter.*

(*What Canst Thou Say?* November 2011 "Death and Dying")

Intimacy in the Journey with God

The longest way to God, the indirect;
lies through the intellect.
The shortest way lies through the heart:
Here is my journey's end and here its start.

The Book of Angelus Silesius, translated by Frederick Franck
Contributed by John Surr (August 2009 "Body Prayer")

In a marriage of true minds there is both passion and cleaning up the spilled oatmeal; both unrelenting pain and deep comfort, questioning and certainty.

Beth Schobernd shares a graced moment as her family gathers for the marriage of her son. Rhonda Pfaltzgraff-Carlson is sustained by God the Comforter, and Carolyn Wilbur Treadway's working life is blessed and inspired by an encounter with her future self. Anne Scherer shares her sense of God's Self with us.

Deborah L. Shaw experienced quaking as being shaken like a piece of silk in a gentle breeze. Evelyn Miranda-Feliciano washes dishes with God as close Companion. Mary Satterfield learns to let go of the outcome of a meeting and let God. Rhonda Ashurst launches a new phase of her working life by creating a sacred workplace.

Jennifer Elam dances with God leading every step. Charleen Krueger experiences honey from the sky as light and softness and peace. Janet Ferguson asks if evil really exists. For Linda Theresa, the pain of her illness never stops, but grace takes precedence in her experience; and Judith Favor senses God's ineffable presence.

Helen Siciliano is enveloped into a divine love that is in everything and everyone. Joyce B. Adams encounters Jesus as the eternal "I am;" and Hazel

Jonjak feels an all-encomnpassing freedom and affinity between herself and the universe. Marty (Verna) Neidigh learns about ministering to the "least of these" as her mother serves tramps from the trains on the tracks across the field from their house.

William Mueller meditates on the life of the Beloved Disciple, while Diann Herzog is inspired to walk as a child of Light. Sadie Vernon learns to trust her dreams and visions. Marcia Jones is comforted in the very moment of her husband's death; and Lillian Heldreth shares with us the moment when her mother's spirit leaves her body,

Join our authors in their sometimes-gritty journey through a life devoted to loving God.

Grace by the Sea

Beth Schobernd

Typically the event marking the touch of grace is short-lived, fleeting, even if the impact is long-term. One instance of receiving grace, however, lasted four days. In September 2004, my son was married in Charleston, South Carolina. Our extended family, 16 of us, stayed in a beach house a few miles down the coast. Renting the beach house seemed the best way to care for the needs of a crowd who ranged in age from 21 months to 87 years. Some of us saw each other once or twice a year, but we were rarely all together as we were for those four days.

I should have expected our time there to be unusual. It was my first close experience with an ocean, and I was awed by the power and mystery of the Atlantic. The house we rented was the only one of its size in town, and in the entire month of September it was available only for the exact four days we needed it. The week of the wedding saw one of the few stretches of nice weather in a fall plagued by hurricanes.

Not long after we arrived, I came to realize that this was to be a special time for my family. It was as if time slowed down at the beach house. All of us relaxed and let the sea spray wash away whatever cares we had. We found ourselves staying up late and rising early just so we could spend more time together. The younger generations got to know each other better, and the older generations deepened their ties. The favorite attractions for everyone were the eight large rocking chairs on the front porch. It seemed there were always people in them, rocking and visiting, from early in the morning until late at night.

In this idyllic setting it also became very obvious that the oldest generation was failing. My mother, in particular, experienced periods of confusion and weakness, even falling once when she got up during the night. We learned this was not a new phenomenon for Mom but increasingly common. Since my father was nearly blind and deaf, Mom was the caretaker in their relationship. This deterioration in her abilities worried all of us. Both Mom and Dad are fiercely independent, so any help would have to be delicately offered and provided. My sister, my cousin and I spent long hours talking about "what if" but managed to do little beyond recognizing the problems. The aging of my parents had always been something I put off thinking about, but here it was staring me in the face and it would not be ignored. I wasn't sure I was up to the challenge.

Slowly, I came to realize that grace was also a guest in the beach house. There could be no other explanation for the sense of peace and calm acceptance I experienced. The gift of grace was two-fold. Our family was given the opportunity to strengthen our bonds in the face of the impending loss of our elders. I was given comfort and strength, and assured that God would be with me no matter what the future might bring. As my parents' health has continued to fail, I am still held by that gift of grace.

Our son and daughter-in-law's wedding was beautiful, a celebration in keeping with their beliefs and personalities. But the wedding, our whole purpose for being there, almost became secondary to the events that transpired at the beach house and the gifts we were given. It was a holy time.

Beth Schobernd *is a member of Clear Creek Meeting, McNabb, Illinois. She is wife, mother, grandmother, and librarian. She recently served as Recording Clerk for Illinois Yearly Meeting.*

(*What Canst Thou Say?* May 2006 "Changed by Grace")

An Encounter with the Comforter

Rhonda Pfaltzgraff-Carlson

A few years ago, while I was taking a spirituality course, we were encouraged to try the spiritual practice of *lectio divina*. I chose to read *Mark* 4:35-41, the story of Jesus and his disciples being in a boat at night during a storm. In the story, the disciples are fearful, so they wake Jesus up. In response, he calms the storm and notes their inability to trust. They respond with terror and awe. The verse that stood out to me in particular was, "Teacher, don't you care that we are going to drown?" (*Mark* 4:38b, SV).

I repeated the text to myself, then noticed myself getting bored. I remembered from the reading we had done about *lectio divina* that this type of reaction was a type of avoidance, so I refocused on the text. Then I began to daydream about a theology student whom I liked. In that fantasy, I was saying to the person, "You must be really brave to be doing what you are doing. You are opening yourself up and risking that everything is going to change, yet you trust that there is something about God that you trust so much that you are willing to take this risk. You are very brave."

Surprisingly, I realized that the words that I had spoken to my friend were really for me. I was moved to tears of gratitude. The message was a blessing that I didn't expect but was very welcome given the difficulties that I was experiencing during my life at the time.

Then I felt a need to cry. I hesitated to do so, but I did anyway. A precious exchange followed between myself and God that helped me to grasp that I was God's daughter. I was led to a sense of belonging to God and to the human family that surprised me. I encountered feelings that were new to me.

This experience did not change me. It just brought me face to face with my internal condition. On this occasion, as with others, I heard messages that were comforting to me or helped me to understand my struggles; however, I was not able to internalize what I heard in a way that led to change.

Looking back, now with a better understanding of myself, I can see that my subconscious mind would not allow me to believe what God was saying to me. I could consciously understand it and feel blessed by it, but I could not integrate the meaning of the words into my internal representation of myself. I needed to heal psychologically so that the spiritual reality to which I had access could become part of myself and my relationship with God.

Like the disciples, I am with God, but I am also fearful. I don't really believe that Christ is with me; that really there is nothing to worry about. I long for Christ to calm the storm, to create in me a place of profound stillness. Nevertheless, I hold onto the idea that once again I too will walk on dry land.

Rhonda Pfaltzgraff-Carlson's *regular spiritual practice is a loose combination of Centering Prayer and Rex Ambler's* Experiment with Light, *which she has practiced for over five years. "These practices help and allow me to be open to God's word. My life's work is to be God's instrument. In addition to waiting on God, I care for my husband and children."*

(*What Canst Thou Say?* August 2013
"Literature as Revelation")

Birthed Into Grace

Carolyn W. Treadway

Several years ago, early in my training to become a personal life coach, we trainees were guided through visualizing our future selves. Usually guided imagery doesn't take me anywhere, but this one was different, powerful, beautiful. Entering this visualization, I never dreamed it would be a profound spiritual experience. But it was.

Guided from present time and place into interstellar space, and back down to somewhere on Earth twenty years hence, I became acquainted with my future self—myself twenty years from now. After seeing the beautiful surroundings and the home of my dreams in which she lived, I saw my future self clearly, and began to get acquainted with her. *She was beautiful— erect, silver haired, graceful, flowing, calm, smiling, spacious, connected, generous, compassionate.* I loved her immediately! A wise woman and respected elder indeed, she touched my heart deeply and opened my vision of who I might eventually be able to become.

At the close of the visualization, we were to ask future-self her name. What came through to me were two names, Graceful and Gracious. I didn't know which. Processing this exercise with a partner, we were both moved when I named my future self Grace, the common denominator of both names I'd been given for her. But Grace was still an abstraction, very much my *future* self, far into the distant future, and as far from me as if we were on opposite sides of the Grand Canyon. We were instructed to use our future self as a resource for our coaching. It sounded like a good idea, but I didn't know how.

Later that day I was coached in a practice session by a training colleague young enough to be my son. Soon he called upon Grace (my future self) to offer her suggestions. I (Carolyn) made comments, but they were abstract and lifeless. He asked to speak to Grace, and I replied that she wasn't here, she was way over there in space and distant time. He asked me to show him Grace, here and now. What would she be doing right now if she were present? *Dancing!* (The word fell out of my mouth.) My young coach rose, pulled me to my feet, and started dancing with me, around and around the room. It was amazing! I moved ever more freely and spiritedly. During this dance, I realized that Grace *was already* present, right here and now! *She was me and I was her!*

In those moments, something shifted in the ground of my being. The Grand Canyon gap between me and Grace disappeared. It was truly a moment of grace, where Grace was birthed, and Grace birthed me into Her. These moments for me were perhaps like Helen Keller's *waaah moments*, the moments when Helen comprehended that Teacher Annie's motions, signing into her hand, actually meant something—meant the *waaaater* from the pump gushing over her hands. From that moment on, a whole new world opened up for Helen. My world changed, too, from knowing that Grace was *already* within me, from knowing inexplicably that Grace and I were already one. Of course I have long known the fundamental Quaker tenet of *that of God in every one*. But this was a visceral knowing, not a head knowing. Truly I was gifted by grace in these moments.

Grace's gifts have not left me since that day. Moment by moment, I can tune in to Grace's presence or absence in me, or to whether or not Grace is being expressed through me. Once awakened, I can no longer *not* know when I am in, or not in, a state of grace. Day by day, I am very often *not* Grace, not gracious, not even graceful. Still, Grace guides me, and constantly invites me into a state of being which I glimpsed so profoundly in my own future self twenty years hence. That vision draws me toward her. Would that I could become her! Would that I could truly express Grace here and now!

Quakers might call my future-self visualization an experience of being in the Light, or having the Inner Light illuminated by grace. Many have had such experiences. For me, there is now a vision, and an understanding, of what it looks like and feels like to be in a state of grace (or in the Light). This guides my days and illuminates my path. Now I am so aware of when I do, and do not, act as Grace. My coaching colleagues call me Coach Grace. It takes only hearing that name to invite me back into the state of being which I experienced in that training exercise: the state of Grace, and the state of being graced by grace. From the place of grace so much more is possible, even in the most mundane dimensions of ordinary daily life. For the opportunities to learn this, I am most grateful. Grace invited me, and continues to invite me, to live up to the Light I have. Now I believe that as I do, more *will* be granted me. May grace gift you too!

Carolyn Wilbur Treadway *is a lifelong Friend and personal life coach living in Normal, Illinois.*

(*What Canst Thou Say?* May 2006 "Changed by Grace")

128 ▶ *Intimacy with God*

Communication with God, with Spirit

Anne Scherer

This drawing was my Christmas card last year (*above*). It was a spiritual experience to create, as happens whenever I sit down before a blank sheet of paper, whether it is to write, draw, or paint. Whenever I go outside with my camera, I look not only with my eyes but with a sense of something far more great—a Presence.

Is that presence a communication with God, with Spirit? Is it mystical? Perhaps, I do not know. All I know is that it is there and it is very real.

I know this because when I cannot do my artwork for whatever reason, whether it be writer's block or just not making or taking the time, I feel a distinct difference in myself and in my soul. Because that Presence that I feel when I am creating is deeply felt, deep within.

Anne Scherer *is an artist, poet and writer. She attends Rochester Friends Meeting in Rochester, Minnesota.*

(*What Canst Thou Say?* August 2011 "Creativity and Mysticism")

Spirit Poured on Flesh
Deborah L. Shaw

We are the Body of Christ
Birthing, feeding, touching, weeping
We are the Body of Christ
Mending, bleeding, healing, dancing
Glorify God in our bodies
Dance with God through our lives

My dear friend Michele Tarter proposed the idea to me that we travel together in spiritual pilgrimage to the 1652 country of England the following summer. My initial reaction was to scoff at the idea, knowing that I didn't have the funds for such an excursion. Michele responded by challenging me to open myself to the miraculous possibilities that abound for those that live in "that life and power." I cannot say that I accepted that challenge in a wholly conscious way, but I know that it did work on me and work in me. ...

Late in March of 1998, I was sitting in meeting for worship at Friendship Friends Meeting. The meeting had been going about 40 minutes when I began to quake. I was aware of a spoken message forming, which is somewhat unusual for me, as I most often sing in meeting for worship. I went through my normal process of testing the leading and trying to discern if the message was just for me, or was one that I was to share. I felt clear, stood and spoke, then sat down. The difference was that I continued to quake—this quaking continued even after meeting closed and the announcements were being given. My mother was visiting at the time and was sitting behind me and she had noticed the quaking continuing. After meeting she asked me, "Where did thee go?" I had no answer at that time. Over five years have passed since the onset of this quaking and it has seemed important to record its manifestations and subtleties and what conclusions I have drawn as I continue to ponder it. ...

This is one of the sweetest and most precious experiences I have ever known of Spirit poured on flesh. I had been wrestling with God about a behavior that I knew was not in harmony with God's will. I was at the place where I wasn't even yet willing to be willing to take it into prayer. As I walked and prayed one morning I finally said, "OK, I admit I might not be right." The minute I said that, I felt as if I had been oh-so-gently lifted by the top of my head and oh-so-gently shaken—like a piece of silk in the gentlest of breezes—so that the ripple went from the top of the piece to the bottom—and in that ripple I felt each one of my cells shift and realign—like so many iridescent fish scales adjusting to the movement of the fish. As I write this I can feel it again, and it moves me to tears. It expresses such gentle and particular care of me that it is beyond belief—and yet I believe.

Deborah L. Shaw is a recorded minister and a member of Friendship Friends Meeting, North Carolina Yearly Meeting (Conservative). Spiritual expression in art, music, and literature is of particular interest to her. She is Worship and Discernment Coordinator/Assistant Director of Friends Center at Guilford College. This is an excerpt from her essay, "In My Body," written for School of the Spirit in 2003. Deborah's entire inspiring and thought-provoking essay is in the archives on our website as the Supplemental (#2) August 2009 <whatcansthousay.org/archives-80-61>.

(*What Canst Thou Say?* August 2009 "Body Prayer")

~~~~~~~~~~~

Lord, Did You Also Wash Dishes?

Evelyn Miranda-Feliciano

It was a querulous question.

Here I was, trapped before a sink stacked with dishes, pots and pans that I had to wash three times a day, seven days a week, forty-eight weeks a year. So deep was my grudge, I even took the pains of multiplying the days by the number of years since I got married—16,060 days of cleaning up, soaping, rinsing, wiping, stacking almost the same plates, the same spoons, saucers, cups and glasses (admittedly, many had been broken and replaced through the years), the same banged-up pans, the same dented pots. Was there no way to escape washing all these?

It was a question smoldering with resentment.

Why, a hubby could just burp and leave the table scratching his well-filled tummy, lounge on a sofa, pick his teeth contentedly while the wife stays to take care of the after-meal mess! She needs to be adept in shifting gears from cooking to serving, and now to cleaning up! To the credit of my own husband (God bless him!), he is responsible for scouring off the soot on our kettles and woks to shininess—the ones we use for cooking in our "dirty kitchen" (an open-fire kitchen area where wood is used, a common feature in Asian households to save on electricity). Despite that help sparing me from having chipped, blackened fingernails, I still groused. The world is not fair!

And, for some time, I took it out upon other writers better situated than I was. Once in an international conference of writers, artists and publishers, I shared the podium with a male non-Filipino writer from the USA. "What it takes to be a writer" was the theme; our audience was young aspiring writers. My partner narrated his daily routine as a professional novelist: He would have his devotions first thing in the morning, then he jogged around for exercise, ate a hearty breakfast and exactly at 8:00, he would head for the garage where he had his private den. There, he would write to his heart's delight—uninterrupted and oblivious to the world—until he thought he had written enough for the day.

That was exactly my ideal picture of a Christian writer. But where was I most times? In the market, haggling over the price of fish early in the morning. Or in a long commute by public bus for a speaking date. Or standing there washing dishes! When people called me a writer I would laugh.

It was a question bristling with self-importance.

I wanted special treatment from God because I was writing about and for him. I wanted to be excused from doing the menial, the seemingly unimportant. All I wanted was to concentrate on what I perceived as significant and honorable. Washing greasy dishes was definitely not one of them.

With this crumpled, grudging frame of mind, my clatter was unusually loud. I swished and swashed, flooding the tabletop near the sink. In the clashing of silverware and clanging of pans, the Lord's voice came.

"I even washed dirty, smelly feet, didn't I?" The answer came softly, in a clear voice that tapped gently in my heart, heard by my inner ear. I paused, startled, holding a soaped-up glass. Why, the Lord spoke to me! Clear as a bell. Gentle as the passing breeze, cooling my heated-up spirit. His tone was tender and understanding, unsullied by any recrimination. He did not shame me or make me feel guilty for asking what seemed a silly question. I think he was smiling right beside me, amused by my frowning face and splashing about. Truly God is remarkable in his ways!

With the realization of his presence right beside me, my grousing turned to joy; my resentment and self-importance turned to awe. Jesus washed dishes! Surely he must have in his lifetime. Being the eldest child of Joseph and Mary, he must have been his mother's errand boy. Did not the narrative say, "So Jesus grew both in height and wisdom, and he was loved by God and by all who knew him"? (Luke 2:52, NLT). Doing the dishes could be one of those tasks that made Mary love this mysterious son of hers more, whose secrets she kept in her heart. For if it were not so, it would have been most unnatural for the Lord to wash his disciples' feet towards the end of his life. No one volunteered to do this servant's duty among them except him, their Master. Not only was the Lord Christ used to washing things; he came purposely to cleanse people of their sins by shedding his blood on the cross on their behalf. Yes, he has cleansed me through my faith in him, and he is not done with me yet.

"Thank you, Lord," I said aloud, grinning. The revelation freed me from smallness. The truth that the Lord Christ, the Savior of the world and Creator of the Universe, washed dishes and human feet is enough reason for me and all the washers in the world, especially women, to sing and do a jig while doing our work.

This means nothing is too low or menial for the children of God to do. Every place, including that space before the kitchen sink, is holy ground. Every task, including scouring the pot's bottom, is a holy task. I am impelled by his love to do everything excellently, whether washing dishes or writing, because Christ, my Lord, stands alongside me—not merely as a spectator, but as one who had done the task himself. I must do everything for God; "and so even the meanest of tasks is clad with glory," as William Barclay puts it.

From the experience I learned to ask God any question that bugs my mind and disturbs my spirit. At times, his answer comes quite quickly, and at other times, he keeps me waiting and guessing. But he answers, nevertheless. I do think that our Lord is very much open to engaging us in a discussion. Job challenged him and Habakkuk peppered him with questions. Both came away stronger in their faith and became more intimate with him and his ways.

The glasses gleamed as I lifted each one from the water and laid them carefully on a towel-lined tray. My plates sparkled ready for use again. I walked from the sink quieted and humbled, but smiling. I just had a conversation with God right at my kitchen sink! Awesome.

Evelyn Miranda-Feliciano *has not stopped asking God questions, though politely and with reverence. Writing from the Philippines, her "Christianity in Cities" is included in the 2009* Atlas of Global Christianity, *1910-2010 by the University of Edinburgh Press.*

(*What Canst Thou Say?* August 2011 "Creativity and Mysticism")

One Thing I Have Asked of the Lord
Mary Satterfield

Message given at 11am Meeting for Worship, Eleventh Month 11, 2012:

> One thing I have asked of the Lord;
> this is what I seek:
> that I may dwell
> in the house of the Lord
> all the days of my life;
> to behold the beauty of the Lord
> and to seek him in his temple.

As I go about my life, I try to remember that God is not only here in the meetinghouse, but also in my workplace, in my garden, and with me as I do chores at home. When I remember this during times of difficulty, I want to stop and ask, "What does God have in mind for me here? What is God trying to teach me?" And then, once again, I am aware of God's presence.

Yesterday at the Friends House Board Meeting I was clerking for the second time. We had a full agenda, and two and a half hours to work through all the agenda. I felt well prepared; I had prepared the agenda and reviewed items. Although concerned about the many items and the lack of time, I had done my best to release it to God so that God could work through me. As the meeting started, items took longer than I expected, and issues arose where I had not envisioned controversy. The process of working through several additional issues meant that there was no way we would be able to finish in the time allotted. With the permission of the Board, we extended the meeting by 30 minutes, heard oral reports on important topics, and concluded the meeting.

Afterwards, I was in a foul mood. It seemed to me that all my planning had been for naught and several of the reports I really wanted to get to had been ignored. I headed home with my head down and with no idea what to do next.

Within a mile of being on the road, the thought occurred to me of how tightly I was holding onto the outcome of the Board meeting; how tightly my mental fist was around the results of the meeting—based on my own presupposition of how it should go. I had done my best to let go and let God run the meeting through me, but somehow at some point I had invested in my outcome and not God's. God had a different plan and I was internally fighting with God over which outcome was better.

When I realized that, I laughed. Of course, God's outcome was better; I knew that. The strange thing was that it took several more miles before I could mentally pry my grasping fingers from around the outcome and release it. It was as if I didn't want to be happy with the outcome unless it was my own; I didn't want to let go; it was mine. It reminded me of the four-year-old I once was, determined to get her way even though it wasn't a good way.

Once I realized that I was so invested in the outcome of the meeting and was able to release it, I began to look back over the events of the meeting and see God at work. Some of the unexpected items had raised up work that really needed to get done; "what wants to happen," I've heard it called. God was there all along, and I was able to see his presence once I was able to look past my own agenda.

I wonder what God has in mind for us here? What lesson is God teaching me in this?

Please, God, help me remember this in the midst of things next time!

Mary Satterfield is a scientist and a member of Sandy Spring Monthly Meeting in Sandy Spring, Maryland, near Washington, DC.

(*What Canst Thou Say?* February 2013 "Prophetic Vision")

Creating a Sacred Workplace
Rhonda Ashurst

I'm sitting in my new office, contemplating this workplace I recently created. It is in an historic, red brick building close to a park. There is an elm tree outside my second-story window, green leaves fluttering in a summer breeze. The fountain my friend Denise made for me chitters happily as water spills down the rocks and seashells we found to make it. Paintings created by the hands of my friends and family hang on the walls. My beloved books sit in shelves next to my folding table desk. I draped the table in a Native American motif fabric to hide the cheap plastic. In front of me are two rocking chairs facing each other—one for me, one for my guest.

I'm not entirely sure what I'm doing here. When I tell the other professionals in the building that I have an office upstairs, but I'm not sure what I will offer, they raise their brows and look at me sideways.

I'd like to tell them, "God told me to get an office. So, I did. I'm awaiting further instructions."

I used to be a psychotherapist. I closed my practice three years ago, too burned out to continue. Since then I've had a gnawing sense that I abandoned my life purpose. It is always there lurking in the shadows of my heart. A few months ago it burst forth like water puncturing the wall of a dam.

I remember when it happened. I had been working from home, running the office of a real estate investing company I own with my husband. Working with each other at home was taking over our entire married life. We sat down together and talked about making changes. Out of my mouth came, "I think I want an office again." It had been an unvoiced thought, lying beneath the surface of my conscious mind. I looked up for his reaction, afraid of what I might see.

He laughed, "What? Isn't making sales brochures and answering the phone giving you a sense of meaning and purpose?" He then proceeded to explore my idea, encouraging me and suggesting I offer my new work as a gift or for a small donation. "Let our company pay for it," he said. "If it is God's will, God will provide a way."

Two months later I'm in the exact office that I envisioned in that moment. It has flowed easily in the way I've come to associate with spirit-driven aspirations. I know that I am supposed to be here, even if I don't know why.

I notice a vision emerging for this workplace. I want it to be a sacred space where the unspoken and tender dreams of individual spirits can be nurtured into reality. This workplace is not about diagnoses, medications, treatment plans, administrative paperwork, government agencies, insurance companies, or expert opinions. This workplace is about supporting possibilities and potentialities, honoring gifts, honing strengths, increasing awareness, sharing truth and facing obstacles with courage.

I struggle to make a brochure explaining this, without placing it in a limiting box of bullet-pointed definitions. I want God's guidance to be able to flow freely through me and this workplace. Too many of my workplaces have been drained of spirit by impossible-to-meet productivity demands, confining rules and restrictions, useless paperwork, and ruthless risk management policies. I will not allow that to happen here.

So, for now, I sit and wait for the next unfolding and I work on trusting the process of this emerging workplace.

Update—Three Months Later

When I wrote this piece for WCTS, it was an exploration of a nebulous idea. Over the summer my vision has crystallized into a life coaching practice. I've always been intrigued by this approach to helping people create the life they long for deep within themselves. I even bought a book about it when I closed my psychotherapy practice. I had loaned it to a friend, who found it this summer while she was moving and returned the book to me. I re-read it in a heated rush, suddenly clear this was the path I wanted to take.

This decision helped me to move forward with business cards and brochures. The brochure became a list of open-ended questions rather than bullet-pointed definitions. Then our real estate investments, which we depend on for income, did not sell as expected over the summer. Suddenly, we were faced with a need for income from other sources.

This crisis led me to revisit the original idea of offering my services for donations. I came to see this turn of financial events as an opportunity to examine my beliefs about the value of my work, and issues around charging for it. I increasingly see what I do as an exchange of energy, and part of that exchange involves money (another form of life energy).

I had barely finished my brochures and business cards, when I began receiving calls inquiring about my services. The fascinating part is that I hadn't distributed anything yet, or placed any ads! One man heard about me from a local business owner, whom I don't even know. Another found me through our real estate website. A third "heard through the grapevine" that I might be practicing again. Now I know God has a hand in this!

As I sit with my clients in this sacred workplace, I feel Spirit move through me in the old ways, using me as an instrument. I remember what I love about this work, and I come to it with a renewed commitment to take care of myself, so I don't have to leave it again. I am reminded that the most sacred workplace is within us and it is vital to honor, respect and nurture ourselves.

Rhonda Ashurst *is a life coach in Alamosa, Colorado. She is a spiritual universalist and feels closest to God when in nature.*

(*What Canst Thou Say?* February 2007 "Spirituality in the Workplace")

Dancing with God

Jennifer Elam

*Dear God, you lead;
I don't know how.
I am better at following;
Sometimes I don't know
 how to do that either.*

*God says, "Write."
I don't know how.
I write. And it is good.*

*God says, "Pray."
I don't know how.
I pray. And it is good.*

*God says, "Paint."
I don't know how.
I paint. And it is good.*

*God says, "Teach."
I don't know how.
I teach. And it is good.*

*God says, "Call."
I don't know how.
I call. And it is good.*

*God says, "Move to a
 different place."
I don't know how.
I re-locate. And it is good.*

*God says, "Speak in
 vocal ministry."
I don't know how.
I speak. And it is good.*

*God says, "Advocate for the
 children."
I don't know how.
I advocate. And it is good.*

*God says, "Dance."
I don't know how.
I dance. And it is good.*

*God says, "Dance as Worship."
I don't know how.
I dance as worship. And it is
 good.*

*God says, "Dance with Me in
 Quaker Meeting for Worship."
I don't know how.
I struggle. I try. I dance a few
 times. I falter. My dance
 becomes more rigid. My life
 no longer dances. I pray,
 "God, give me the strength."
 Strength and possibility do not
 come. "God, where are you?"
 The dance stops flowing. I
 falter further.*

*Dear God, you lead;
I don't know how.
I am better at following;
Sometimes I don't know
 how to do that either.*

Jennifer Elam is psychologist, painter, writer, and dancer, the author of *Dancing with God through the Storm: Mysticism and Mental Illness.*

(*What Canst Thou Say?* August 2009 "Body Prayer")

Honey from the Sky
Charleen Krueger

About a year before my father died, I began to have experiences that spoke to my condition. As I was walking on a sunny sidewalk, doing last minute errands prior to flying across the country to see my father, perhaps for the last time, I was stopped mid-stride. A feeling of absolute serenity poured over me like honey from the sky. My arms opened to my sides; my face turned upward, my eyes closed, and I smiled—all of it as involuntary as being jolted to my feet by ministry in meeting. This happened in an airport as I worried if I would make it to his side in time, and again as I sat quietly with him during his last week of life on earth.

A second kind of experience after my father died was seeing a dark shadow-person shape from the corner of my eye and feeling a presence. No one frightening, just an unannounced visitor. I do not have the feeling this is my father, nor have I received any teaching or messages. There is just someone there, observing.

Now there is a new experience—when I am walking and being still inside, sometimes I walk through a liquid sheet of light. It comes to me, not I to it. Suddenly I am on the other side. Once there were shadow figures there—a tall dark standing shape seen from the side and a kneeling red one, seen from the back. The tall one is solicitous of the kneeling one, a teacher with a pupil. But usually, there is only light and softness and peace.

There has been a concurrent gift with these experiences—acceptance without puzzlement or distress.

Charleen Krueger *is a member of Claremont, California, Meeting. She reports that her main spiritual interest is incorporating spiritual practice into daily life.*

(*What Canst Thou Say?* February 2006 "Touched by the Spirit")

> "The Gospel of Philip ... the conviction that God's spirit constantly contends against Satan. Instead of envisioning the power of evil as an alien force that threatens and invades human beings from outside, the author of Philip urges each person to recognize the evil within and consciously eradicate it." —Elaine Pagels
> (*The Origin of Satan*. Vintage Books, NY, 1995, p. 176-77.)

Does Evil Exist?

Janet Ferguson

For years I have wrestled with the suggestion that there is no evil. How can this be in the face of all the war, crime, cruelty and depravity around us? I have mulled over the assertion in *A Course in Miracles*: "Nothing real can be threatened; nothing unreal exists."

To me some of the teachings of the ancient Hindu Upanishads throw light on this perplexing problem. They also assert that nothing unreal exists, that the seeming evil around us is what Hindus call "maya," the illusory world of the senses in which we are eternally embroiled. Above all this "creaturely activity," as Friends call it, is the supreme Self, the everlasting, infinite Brahman, called God, Allah, Ultimate Reality, All-That-Is, Spirit, or whatever. In a 1931 address to the American people, Gandhi said, "whilst everything around me is ever changing, ever dying, there is underlying all that change a living power that is changeless, that holds all together, that creates, dissolves, and recreates. That informing power of spirit is God."

Perhaps evil is a creation of the human mind, as explanation of all that dismays us in our world. In her inspiring, anonymously published book, *Christ in You*, Alice Mortly asserted that evil is designed to prod us into growth, as a seed is prodded into growth by the action of the soil, sun and rain. Adlai Stevenson pointed out that there is no evil in an atom; surely the great motions of the cosmos do not involve evil. Even the bewildering destruction of life by creatures feeding on other creatures can be seen as part of a larger plan.

I am increasingly inclined to believe that evil is a human concept, not part of the divine order of things. The Apostle Paul wrote to the Romans, "Be not overcome by evil, but overcome evil with good." And George Fox told us, "I saw that there was an ocean of darkness and death, but an infinite ocean of light and love which flowed over the ocean of darkness. In that also I saw the infinite love of God."

Janet Ferguson *is a member of Atlanta Friends Meeting, a writer and activist.*

(What Canst Thou Say? November 2006 "Evil")

When Does Grace Enter?

Linda Theresa

For me, grace is when I see, feel or know things beyond the normal ways. Grace is a glimpse of God. Maybe it's easier to say what grace is not: I'm no longer in my small ego-driven world full of discursive thinking. Instead, the heart of grace is beyond time, space, and concepts, although miraculous events, wondrous insights and blissful sensations often form the most lasting impressions.

After my initial experience of grace, I hungered for more, and was even angry for months when the same method of prayer didn't yield the same experience of grace day after day. Through repeated mistakes, I've learned that the sure way not to have an experience of grace is to expect God to follow my greedy, anxious tantrums. I did, however, go on to have many numinous experiences when I caught glimpses of the divine. Also, I felt intuitively that there was some commonality of behaviors, traits, attitudes or conviction that opened the way for these experiences to happen. I pored through all my old journal entries and created a chart of all the experiences and the feelings and behaviors preceding them. Can you tell I used to be a business systems analyst?

It's now been several years since I created that chart and who knows where it is, but its impact continues to serve me to this day, because it was really a model for living a God-centered life. I still struggle; I'm no saint. More than anything, I hope this article is of some use to you and to me, because I truly believe we are milliseconds away from feeling divine grace each moment of the day. I've gone through periods where God's presence was deeply felt throughout each day, even when I was engaged in everyday chitchat or in severe pain gasping for breath....

Whatever we seek we shall find. Even my greedy, anxious anger at not experiencing God's grace was a plea that God honored. One begins to learn what attitudes, beliefs and actions draw one closer and which ones lean toward separation. It's a world where paradoxes abound, but in their midst truth is known.

I'll give you an example. Take any duality that gives you some concern, such as one person wanting a more intimate relationship and another wanting more space. Now pretend you are a person at one end of the spectrum and have decided to change to be at the other end of the spectrum. Write down all the feelings and concerns that come up. Now pretend you are at the other end of the spectrum and must change totally. Again write down a long list of how that might feel. Lastly, find where the lists are similar, and here's the hard part: sit with that feeling until you transcend it. The only way to transcend it is to fully feel every nuance of it. Although it feels like you may die, it's really only the belief in the ego that dies. Suddenly, you see the truth with indescribable clarity.

When we are open to knowing and accepting anything, we enter sacred ground. Whether we are allowing emotions, ideas, or even physical pain, we create an openness where a shift is often made. When we create enough silence, we will hear. When we make friends with the opposite of what we usually do and believe, we open a gateway. The kingdom of God lies within you. Trust it, relax into it, and God's grace will enter.

Linda Theresa, *Alamosa, Colorado, was unable to type due to chronic pain. She sent this handwritten article to editor Mariellen Gilpin, who was typing it when the phone call came that Linda had died. She practiced Vipassana Buddhism as a means of living at peace with pain. Always upbeat on the phone, she lived her truth to the very end. Thank you, Linda.*

(*What Canst Thou Say?* May 2006 "Changed by Grace")

An Ineffable Presence
Judith Favor

My first direct experience of Jesus happened on a sunny September morning in 1979, during a meditation retreat at Shasta Abbey. I was thirty-nine years old. A yearning for something more had brought me back for a third helping of sitting meditation. I did not know what I hoped to have happen at the Buddhist retreat center; I could not name what I sought. I only knew that some inchoate longing within me was growing so urgent it could no longer be denied. So I returned to sit in silence with others in a simple meditation hall on the high slopes of Mt. Shasta.

Roshi Jiyu Kennett honored her Buddhist lineage by opening each meditation session with a traditional chant that named a long line of spiritual teachers. I joined in, mispronouncing the unfamiliar Asian names but trying to keep up with the chanted pattern that led us into silence.

Suddenly I was infused with light, lots more light than the autumn sun sent through the zendo window. This light was warmly radiant, bringing a sense of joy that made my heart beat fast, leaving me feeling deeply calm and wildly excited at the same time. *What just happened here?*

Remembering that I had come to Shasta Abbey to practice Buddhist meditation, I tried to turn my attention back to the empty breath, but I could not do it. The light was too intense, the love too overwhelming. Inwardly I heard words that are written on my heart to this day, words from Jesus, the Christ: *These are not your saints. Don't pretend to be Buddhist. Come unto me.*

Did the experience last thirty seconds or thirty minutes? Time dissolved in the ineffable and undeniable presence of love. I felt directly addressed in the same combination of acceptance and challenge that marked Jesus' teachings in the Gospels. The spoken invitation and the soul-stirring warmth combined to convince me I had indeed been touched by the same power that converted fishermen into apostles. The experience set my life on the Way, endeavoring to love God, self and neighbor with all my heart, with all my mind, with all my soul, and with all my strength.

One unexpected and unbidden encounter with the Living Christ, in a Buddhist monastery of all places, set one woman on a course of Christian ministry and lifelong service to the least of these. As a retired pastor in the United Church of Christ, a convinced member of the Religious Society of Friends, a grandmother, seminary teacher and spiritual guide, I sometimes ask: *What gives you hope? What helps you stay aware of the basic wonder and mystery of life?*

For me, it comes through an intentional combination of silent attention and spoken word, solitude and service. I like to imagine the gospel of John starts, *In the beginning was the Silence, and then came the Word.* The unprogrammed worship of Quakers offers me a word-free, doctrine-free zone in which to wait in the Light with others, to rest at the center with Friends.

The ethical teachings of the historical rabbi Jesus appeal to my rational mind. The warm presence of the Risen Christ moves my heart. The energetic vitality of the I AM, Alpha and Omega, is embodied in my bones, blood and vital organs. And my soul responds devotionally to the ultimate universal Source, the Essence of Love.

Judith Favor is a member of Claremont Meeting, is active in Southern California Quarterly Meeting, and offers retreats at Ben Lomond Quaker Center.

(*What Canst Thou Say?* August 2006 "Jesus")

A Love I Could Not Put Into Words

Helen Siciliano

I had been meditating every afternoon for the previous year and a half. On this lovely spring day, upon completing my meditation, I arose with the calmness and peace associated with a lengthy meditative state. I noticed as I looked out the window that I was one with the blades of grass and the rocks in the road. I was enveloped in a love I could not put into words. This divine love was in everything and everyone. At the core of my being I was this love, and so was everyone else.

In this state of grace, there was no right or wrong, no good or bad, no winning or losing, no judgment whatsoever. Fear was nonexistent! There was no death, and I knew that we all live forever. Everyone I met was love. It did not matter what they looked like, behaved like. I was them and they were me. We were all connected. The utter joy was indescribable. The peace and bliss were beyond words. I became aware that a Presence other than what I usually think of as myself was looking through my eyes. I had become one with this infinite awareness that simply sees without judgment. It was the very essence of life, eternal life. I wanted nothing, needed nothing. It was peace that passeth understanding.

For about two weeks I was in this state. During this time I came upon a man who ordinarily I'd have seen as drunk and disheveled, sitting on a curb. I saw his true being. He was love. There was no judgment. He was as worthy as everyone else. He was loved as much as everyone else. I was seeing beyond appearances. I understood that this is our natural state. This is how we are meant to live. It did not matter what I did or had.

There was Joy in every act, every chore, every occasion. Love and joy pervaded everything. The energy of the universe was love and it flowed through us all. We were all a part of this love. We were all one with God. As the Bible taught, we live and move and have our being in him. As Christ taught, the Kingdom of Heaven is within us.

This realization changed me forever. I was in the world but not of it. For two glorious weeks I went to sleep with a smile on my face and awoke smiling in utter joy. On the fourteenth day, I was having a telephone conversation with my mother, and she too had noticed the profound change. I guess on this day I felt I should tell her. When I tried to describe the experience, my ego came back; for the experience was not me but what was coming through me, which could not really be spoken of—there were no words to adequately describe it. The expansion dissipated as suddenly as it had appeared. One cannot take credit for God.

I didn't know what to do. I was now in ordinary reality, or the relative world as I've come to call it, but with the knowledge of the Greater Truth/God. It was the separation all over again, thrown out of the garden. "How do I live like this?" I asked myself. It was most difficult to listen to the world news, to see how we are to each other.

My experience had changed me forever. To know that we were all connected in Spirit, and to have witnessed the oneness of all creation in a state of love and bliss, was to glimpse God. The experience of feeling something other than myself as myself, yet that had its own identity, had changed my perspective on life in a way that is difficult to express.

It was then that I began to search for others who could relate to such a revelation, and I found myself at the University of Connecticut in a support group for people who had had near death experiences, who understood that one can touch the center of one's being without the body dying, but by dying to the self instead. It wasn't long after that my search for a church that exemplified love and unity began, and it was my son, Joe, who led me to First Church of Christ.

So dear friends, as we come to know that we, all of us, are unconditionally loved by the Beloved of all hearts, may we begin to sense our shared oneness with love. As we come to understand that there is but one being that each of us participates in, we may begin to sense our oneness with all. Everyone has been aware of eternal moments, be they in nature, in a child's birth, in listening to sublime music, in glimpses of wonder or in the sudden sense of Presence within us; each a hint of heaven here on earth, of our own consciousness being expanded out into the infinity of oneness that we are. Fear and all its companions have no home here. For in the end, love is all there is! It is my hope that we will one day have Heaven on Earth and live as Christ has taught, loving our neighbors as ourselves. Amen!

Helen Siciliano *retired from banking, has three grown sons, and has been married 48 years. She belongs to First Church of Christ in New London, Connecticut. She began meditating at 45, just as a way to relax.*

(*What Canst Thou Say?* May 2009 "Strangers")

Encounters with Jesus

Joyce B. Adams

When I am alone, sometimes a Presence, like a second breath, has animated the space around me. As I work or walk alone, my concentration yields. I look up to feel the divine breath, intensely concentrated yet unseen and unheard. It is too alive, warm, vibrant to be abstract Spirit. The eternal "I am" has taken individual form. Many speak of meeting Jesus in a mountaintop experience or deep crisis. In truth, I do not base my witness on a particular moment of glory or relief. I experience the fullness of Jesus' presence not in a vision or emotion, but in the unique closeness of the encounter. The Presence is inseparable from what I identify as Self.

Joyce B. Adams, a member of Bloomington, Indiana, Meeting, has a concern for the relationship between spirituality and creativity, contemplation and writing.

(*What Canst Thou Say?* August 2006 "Jesus")

An All-Encompassing Affinity
Hazel Jonjak

It may seem out of character for a Pagan Quaker crone to divulge that her Seeing deepened and radiated with the use of a substance, yet that is the truth in my life. I do remember one spontaneous surreal experience from childhood: *I am sitting on the medium-green linoleum bespangled with large pink and beige roses of my sister's and my upstairs bedroom. I am playing with the furniture and dolls of a homemade dollhouse my mother created of wood and paint. The hinged roof of the dollhouse is folded back, allowing sunshine from the dormer windows of our room to wash the dolls' house, upstairs bedroom, me, and the colorful floor with light. I feel permeated with Golden Something—and feel absolutely serene and open.*

When I was 25, I had another experience which transformed me spiritually. I became friendly with the young hippie couple next door. They were Canadian foster parents, taking in troubled teenagers for an income, but were rather unstable themselves.

At their urging, I at last capitulated to Timothy Leary's "tune in, turn on, and drop out," taking my first tab of LSD. My first acid perception was of the miraculous flow and play of light in and about what had once been an ordinary clear glass doorknob. Light shimmered and prismed into and from the many angles of this magical object. I was eager to step outdoors to see the living world with this fantastic visioning. I stepped out onto their second floor balcony and felt an all-encompassing freedom and affinity between my Hazel-organism and the universe. When my more experienced companions cautioned me to come back in—the balcony was rickety and not to be trusted—I reluctantly re-entered the house. Now I knew if I did stop being Hazel, if I reunited with Creation, that was wonder-full, but my parents would never recover from the shock and loss if I crashed to my death from this shabby building.

It was time for me to leave. I walked on the little roadway to my home, witnessing the catkins on a bush transform from plant-beings to caterpillar-beings within the shifting of an eyelid.

I spent the next few hours in absorbed, borderline-freaky See-ing. The multiple, identical, photograph copies of an unknown stiff young man from the 19th century that I had chosen from an antique store bin and tacked side by side on my living room wall now proved not to be identical. He was just pretending to be the same man in the same pose in each picture. When I washed dirty dishes in the sink I knew this was a sacred task, and I would never again resent the ritual of the cleansing of the dirty dishes. When I at last felt able to go to sleep I crawled into my bed profoundly exhausted, but infinitely wiser than I had been at noon.

Hazel Jonjak appreciates the Inner Light and the peace witness of Friends, and also values sweat lodges and living in the woods for insights and guidance.

(*What Canst Thou Say?* August 2005 "Seeing")

Invited Into the Kitchen
Marty (Verna) Neidigh

Directly across a large field from my family's Plymouth, Indiana farm, trains spewed soot onto our front porch and dropped off tramps who found their way to our back porch, where they apparently knew they'd be invited in for a meal. They were invited into our kitchen where my mother would kindly fix a meal to eat at our kitchen table. However, as I remember, the tramps came one at a time, not in groups. Mother did change to serving the meals on the back porch steps after one fellow dipped his used spoon into our family's sugar bowl! Enough was enough!

In 1965, when we bought my father's family farm near Bremen, Indiana, an upstairs bedroom had long been designated as the tramp room. Apparently tramps were welcome to spend the night in a bed.

Marty (Verna) Neidigh has been married 62 years. Hard of hearing since birth, Marty found her way to South Bend Friends Meeting, Indiana, where her still, small voice told her, "Stay." There she has been accepted, nurtured, loved, eldered, and supported in her accessibility efforts.

(*What Canst Thou Say?* August 2007 "Hospitality")

The Beloved Disciple
God is love (1 John 4:8)
William H. Mueller

These six meditations follow on each of the scriptural passages of the Beloved Disciple. The synoptic gospels tell Jesus' story, but John's gospel, often referred to as "the Quaker gospel," tells God's story through the figure of the man Jesus. In John's gospel Jesus loved a man, the Beloved Disciple. This figure represents Love precedent over Authority (represented by the disciple Peter) in the redemptive life of the Christian (New Jerome Biblical Commentary, 1990, F. J. Moloney "Johannine Theology," pp. 1417-1426 and P. Perkins "The Gospel According to John", pp. 942-985).

In secret he goes with Andrew, unnamed
To follow the Lamb of God.
He, like Andrew, lacks a place to live,
The Rabbi invites the two to come and see*.
                  (John 1:37)

At table, one will deceive the others,
Threatening community.
Authority lacks confidence to ask "Who is it?"
Love leans intimately close to God's heart and does it for him.
                  (John 13:23)

There below the dying Christ,
Stands the mother and his friend.
He commends Love to his mother,
She in turn supports Love's grief.
                  (John 19:26)

Mary Magdala flees the empty tomb,
and tells Authority and Love the Lord is gone.
Love outdistances Authority and looks in the cave,
Authority comes and steps in, helping Love to see.*
                  (John 20:1)

Fishing on the Sea of Galilee with no hope of catch,
A stranger suggests they look to starboard.
There abundance of fish is found,
Love helps Authority to see* it is the Lord.
                  (John 21:7)

While the Rabbi and Authority go on,
Love stays behind.
(This Authority cannot understand.)
It is love that endures, when authority is dead.
                  (John 21:20)

William H. Mueller is a member of St. Lawrence Valley Friends Meeting (Potsdam, New York), an allowed meeting under the care of Ottawa Monthly Meeting, where he is involved in a local prison ministry. He edits a monthly prison newsletter "The Inlook-Outlook Letter".

    (*What Canst Thou Say?* August 2011 "Creativity and Mysticism")

*In Hebrew mythology the verb "to see" denotes the human-God encounter.

Walk as Children of Light

Diann Herzog

Almost from my first meeting for worship, I began having experiences that I couldn't easily explain to myself or others. I hadn't done any background reading on Quakers and hadn't known anyone who was a Quaker. I found my way into a meetinghouse by way of a Historical Society meeting. Just being in the building set something off in me. I felt a strong sense of being called, and was compelled to come back to find out more. I had only been in meeting for worship two or three times when I received the first message, "*Christ is living inside us. He is seeing through our eyes. We carry him in our bodies.*"

I melted, I trembled, I wept; I opened my mouth and let the words come through. I had never heard anyone speak in meeting, didn't yet know that this is a physical manifestation of the Spirit in Quaker worship. Afterwards I felt deeply embarrassed and totally at a loss for explanation. But there was no comfort from the other Friends in meeting that day. I went home thoroughly shaken. I wondered if what had happened was real. At the same time, there was a truth and solidity about the message. I knew whatever it was I had heard and felt was real and true. It was the certainty of the message, how deeply and completely it had spoken to and from my soul, that carried me back to meeting and forward into Quakerism. It has been that soul recognition, that experience of Christ within, that has sustained me.

I consider myself blessed to have come through this and many other intense and powerful experiences without losing myself or my way forward. There are several things that have safeguarded me. Most important is that everlasting Presence that called to me in the first place: that soul within that is my own and yet greater than my own, that tells me I am safe and loved. Next is my husband, who even though he professes to be a non-believer, has listened to every word, every detailed description of my experiences and withheld comment. The act of listening is so very powerful. I can't emphasize that enough. Just to be listened to when I was vulnerable and fragile was a balm to my rawness. Listening is love.

I have also been blessed to have found a couple of experienced and trustworthy Friends who continue to assure me that I haven't lost my mind, that these kinds of experiences aren't unheard of. They have guided me to the right books at the right time. At the beginning of this journey, I had very little knowledge of the *Bible*, but scripture has come to be my touch stone. That is where I find personal guidance, correction and assurance. The first hand experiences of the prophets assure me that, yes, God does speak to us directly at times. The lives and the writings of the disciples affirm my passion for Christ and the living, breathing words of God; the Holy Spirit speaks now in a way I couldn't hear before.

Diann Herzog *is clerk of Fall Creek Meeting, Pendleton, Indiana, and an affiliate member of Stillwater Meeting, Ohio Yearly Meeting (Conservative). She is called to wear plain dress.*

(*What Canst Thou Say?* May 2005 "Spiritual Emergence(y)")

Dreams and Visions

Sadie Vernon

One morning I woke up very sad and my grandmother finally got me to tell her what my tears were about. I had a dream in which I saw my dear Uncle P in a coffin in the parlor. She assured me he was well, that she had heard from him and he would be home soon. I felt better, but so needed to see him. In a few weeks he came and I felt better. Then it happened: a few weeks later he fell ill and never recovered. There he was in that coffin, just as I had seen him. It was devastating to a five-year-old. My grandmother knew I wanted an explanation.

"You have second sight. If you see anything like this again, don't tell everybody. Just tell me. People will want to pay you to tell them what you see. Do not ever get that started."

After leaving home I was made aware whenever a member of my mother's family passed on. At my grandmother's passing I dreamed of angels carrying her away. My Uncle Wallace's death was also made known, as I saw angels carry him away. ...

One morning I woke up after a terrifying dream. I was nervous and afraid to leave the house, though I knew I had to teach school. I was not ill and my class would be waiting. The dream went like this:

I was on my way to school when just at the railway junction I saw a girl on a bicycle and a little dog beside her. Coming from the right was the doctor in his car. He did not, really could not, see the girl coming up the grade. Coming around the left curve was a truck. I could not see it but heard it grinding its way around the slope. As the girl got on the bike with the dog running beside her, she turned almost in the doctor's path and he swerved to avoid her, just as the truck came around the bend. The car bounced against the truck and was turned in the opposite direction. As the truck driver put on his brakes, some men in the back of the truck were flung up and over and some just lay on the ground as though they were dead or injured. I was standing about six inches from the front wheel of the truck with my back against a barbed wire fence.

I really wanted someone to go with me to school. The Senior Matron was very busy; the yard boy was out; and nobody could understand my fear. I finally got the children's matron to agree to go.

We were no sooner in the very spot where I was in the dream when the whole thing went off as I had seen it. The only difference was that in the dream I was alone, but in the event someone was with me! ...

If I lie on my back, I see lots of colors, all colors of the rainbow swirling around. That is the way the visions start, but if I turn over, I can stop it. So, I pile up pillows beside me in bed so I never roll over onto my back. I do not want to see the visions because they relate to the future and I am prepared to live one day at a time. It is going to happen anyway. If I cannot change anything, I do not want to know.

Sadie Vernon *is the only Belizean Quaker. She was Executive Director of the Belize Council of Churches, work supported by Friends United Meeting Missions. This is an excerpt from her autobiography,* In Transit: The Story of a Journey. *Published in 2000 by Producciones de la Hamaca, Judy Lumb, Editor.*

(*What Canst Thou Say?* August 2011 "Creativity and Mysticism")

I Felt His Spirit Leave

Marcia J. Jones

On Thursday, November 8, 2007, the doctor examined my husband Jimmy. He said because Jimmy was young and had a strong heart, he expected him to live a few more days. But something inside of me thought otherwise. I sensed an urgency to hold Jimmy. The hospice nursing staff graciously allowed me to lie down with Jimmy and hold him throughout the day. They moved his catheter and positioned him so we could face each other in his small bed.

During those last two days, I held him tenderly and sang of my love for him. I also sang praise and worship songs that Jimmy knew, and sometimes I sang prayers. I just did what I felt like doing at the time. Countless times I kissed his face and told him I loved him. I held him in my arms, still savoring the magic I had experienced on our first date. I loved being with him. I always had.

Intimacy in the Journey with God

From the first time we had met, Jimmy had always calmed me whenever he held me. Now I was holding him to keep my promise of being there for him when he died. About ten-thirty on the night he would die, I decided I was going to sleep in Jimmy's bed if the staff would allow it. God does all things well. He had a wonderful nurse on duty that night, a real angel. She said that would be fine and to just let her adjust Jimmy's catheter and move him so he would be facing me when I held him.

At 10:40 pm, Snugglebunny got into bed with Snugglebear for one last snuggle. He looked like his old self—my Jimmy. When we retired in 2002, Jimmy weighed 217 pounds and was five feet nine inches tall. Now he weighed only 130 pounds and was only five feet five inches tall, but God let me see my husband as he had been rather than the little shrunken man he had become. Jimmy looked so handsome and seemed at peace.

I couldn't believe my eyes. My Jimmy was back. He seemed peaceful as I held him close. I didn't sing to him; I just snuggled up to him, enjoying the sweet intimacy of our bodies touching. It felt so good—like old times. I relaxed and closed my eyes for a few moments, just savoring the wonderful feeling of holding Jimmy in my arms.

Finally, I opened my eyes and looked at Jimmy. I rubbed his head, kissed him on his forehead, and told him I loved him. Then I put my hand on his chest and said, "Jesus, Jesus, Jesus." On the third "Jesus,' I felt my husband's spirit leave. He simply flew away. It was like the wisp of a butterfly's wings, a mere flutter and gentle breeze. It was faster than I could blink an eye. I still marvel at that night.

I did not want to lose this feeling of being in the presence of a holy God. It felt like the Lord had taken a scrub brush and washed me clean; it was wonderful. I went down to the chapel and called my son Paul while the staff prepared Jimmy for our viewing.

The nurse took us back to Jimmy's room. They had placed a beautiful quilt on him. There was a table at the end of his bed with a lit candle, fresh flowers, family pictures, and the Bible opened to the 23rd Psalm. Paul said, "Mom, he's really gone. I can't feel his spirit like I did earlier. I've always believed in heaven, but I really do now. He's gone. He's free. He's not here. I feel like running down the beach and shouting, 'He's free! He's free!'" We were both so overjoyed we stayed up that night at home and talked about our lives with Jimmy.

from No Greater Love: A Journey through Alzheimer's. *Marcia J. Jones, Xulon Press, 2010, contributed by Dawn Rubbert*

(*What Canst Thou Say?* November 2011 "Death and Dying")

I Think Her Spirit Passed Then

Lillian Heldreth

Anticipatory Grief—I had nearly ten years of it while my mother was slowly slipping away from dementia. It has its advantages, in that if you let it flow in a reasonable manner, it gives you time to work on issues, appreciate the person, and, in the end, feel joy for that person that the suffering is over.

After I'd told my unconscious mother that she was free to go on if called, I began to read to her from the first chapter of John: *And the Word was in the beginning with God, and the Word was God,* with as nearly as possible the cadence my Baptist minister father would have used. Mother rose up in the bed and gave a little cry, and then lay back down, breathing very lightly, whereas before her breath had been heavy. I think her spirit passed then, at the sound of those words. Sometime after that her breathing ceased. I wept then, until I had to make way for the staff, who were due to leave, and did not want anyone else to make her ready for the last journey. Although her mind was virtually gone, her sweet spirit had stayed to the last, and they, too, loved her.

But because so much of my personal grief had come before, on the long drives to and from the nursing home, at her funeral I could speak gladly and in triumph of her long life well-lived, in love and faith. That was the great gift of anticipatory grief.

Lillian Heldreth *attended Urbana-Champaign meeting before moving to Marquette, MI, where she is an elder in a Native American worship community.*

(*What Canst Thou Say?* November 2011 "Death and Dying")

Celebrating Intimacy with God

When we love God with all our heart and with all our strength, then in this love we love our neighbors as ourselves, and a tenderness of heart is felt toward all people, even such who as to outward circumstances are to us as the Jews were to the Samaritans.... In this love we can say that Jesus is the Lord and the reformation in our souls, manifested in a full reformation of our lives, wherein all things are new and all things are of God.   **—John Woolman, Journal**

Mystics choose to walk with God in sickness and in health. They also experience joy.

Bob Barnes celebrates life as rooms become vibrantly alive. Patricia McBee asks only to love God more dearly. Jennifer Elam celebrates Easter, and learns that she can yell at God and know herself loved by God.

Helen Weaver Horn welcomes an April morning. Sally Campbell is joyful that her spiritual gifts were given to be shared. Zarinea Lee Zolivea shares a vision she sees in worship, and James Baker reports God has shown him how to live.

Christine O'Brien faces terminal illness feeling she has received blessings beyond naming. Judy Lumb shares God's humorous way of telling her not to fix other people. Mariellen Gilpin's unitive experiences allow her openly to declare herself horny for God.

Kathleen Maia Tapp celebrates feminine aspects of the Divine. Allison Randall expresses her gratitude in celebration of life with photography. Patricia Reitemeier discovers the Light of God is the oneness of everything. Mike Resman writes of his love for God. Janet Means Underhill gives thanks.

May we all give thanks for our authors' deep sharing of the joy of living in intimate relationship with God.

What Treasures!

Bob Barnes

Living in Northern California means I am blessed with the opportunity of walking to meeting for worship (and many other places, too!) through the flora and fauna of the Gold Rush foothills. Increasingly and happily over the last few years a marvelous phenomenon takes place:

Suddenly I stop (but not so quickly as to stumble!) and find that I'm nearly stunned: Everything has changed.

And nothing has changed.

The shrubs, the trees, the hills, the rocks, the clouds are all the same as they were—except there is a qualitative difference in their colors, even though the colors are just what they were just before the shift. To say it is marvelous is the understatement of the century. Words are too miniscule to carry the weight of the experience. What can I do except gaze in awe, in wonderment at what is happening, to throw my arms wide open, make a little circle dance and over and over exclaim, Thank you, Thank you! Whoever, whatever, wherever you are: Thank you! Thank you! Thank you! (Expressed in as many languages as I can recall.)

And then it passes, more slowly than it began.

These precious flashes—but they are longer than just a flash—occur in other settings as well. Sitting in Meeting, seeing the many familiar faces, sensing those presences as well as knowing their presence in the room. Digging a ditch and being lifted up in the gratitude of hard, heavy, sweaty meaningful work. When I read the call for this message from WCTS the room came vibrantly alive as I glanced over to the card table, the cedar walls, the papers laid out on the carpeted floor.

Oh! What treasures!

Bob Barns *is a member of Grass Valley Meeting in Nevada City, California. He spends as much time in prison as he can—he is a facilitator for Alternatives to Violence. He tries to follow the motto, "if my life does not speak, my words are hollow."*

(*What Canst Thou Say?* August 2005 "Seeing")

To Love Thee More Dearly
Patricia McBee

About a year ago I was at a small conference of Friends who travel in the ministry. It was an occasion steeped in deep worship and deep searching for God's guidance. Reflecting the central themes of the vocal ministry, much of my worship centered around what is the condition of our world? What is God asking of me? Have I been faithful? Do I have the clarity and courage to be faithful to what is put before me?

And then, in the final worship, I sensed a sharp rebuke from the Inward Guide. "Willfulness," it said. "This is willfulness masquerading as submission to God." "Willfulness?" I asked. "Yes, willfulness. It is not about what you can do to save the world or to save the Religious Society of Friends. That all centers around you. Can you center your life around me?"

That started my quest of now several months of trying to learn more about what it would mean to center my life around loving God. Below are excerpts from my journal over this period. As you will clearly see, I'm still a work in progress. Some of the entries are a dialogue between me and the Inward Voice so they move back and forth between referring to me as "I" and as "you."

> Day by day, day by day
> Oh, dear Lord, three things I pray
> To see thee more clearly,
> Love thee more dearly
> Follow thee more nearly, day by day.
>
> The musical Godspell adapted this song from a prayer by St. Richard of Chichester (1197-1253)

March 23, 2004

How does one know God? Spend time with others who know God and ask for an introduction? Give God a call and say "Let's hang out"? Look for God's footprints in all that you see?

At this stage in your spiritual development it is not a matter of merely looking for beauty/harmony/sunshine and saying "There is God." You have to look at it all: the interplay of light and shadow, birth and death, fair weather and storm, the destructiveness of nature as well as the harmonies, human kindness and human cruelty. All are manifestations of God.

This is your task: look at it all, especially the parts you don't want to look at.

156 ▶ Intimacy with God

March 24, 2004

What do I see when I look upon my God? A shower of love for me. I'm beautiful and precious. The whole world, the whole universe is beautiful, precious, magical. Even people who annoy me, beautiful, precious. A gift, not a project.

April 11, 2004

Jesus' eyes of compassion are for me. Jesus looks on me with compassion. There she is, Pat McBee, just as she is. Flawed, fearful, judgmental, at times undisciplined, not able to stay awake and watch with me. Splendid in her desire to love the Breath of Life, in her kindness, her generosity with her time and love, her discipline in doing things thoroughly and well, her willingness (however hesitant) to learn. Just as she is, a child of the Breath of Life, learning to toddle toward her loving parent.

Striving is not needed to earn God's love. When you give up your striving and egotistical worry about whether you're ok, all you have to do is let the compassion flow through you. Open your heart and let it fill and fill, and fill and fill and fill until it can hold no more and begins to overflow out of your eyes, out of your mouth, out of your pores. When you're finding it hard to love someone, just remember that Jesus is in there ahead of you.

April 15, 2004

Who is my God?

All of it is my God: Gray skies today, a friend's kindness, more U.S. deaths in Iraq, people in Nicaragua cutting down their shade tree to have fuel to cook their beans. This is what it means to look upon God—it means look at it all, rumbling and churning, sending out flashes of beauty and cries of pain. This is the day the Breath of Life has made, rejoice and be glad in it.

How does one look at God and not die? You can't. This is an exercise in refining the ego. The idea is for you to die to yourself, to become more transparent to compassion.

Feelings have emerged: fear, shame, hurt, anger, rage, confusion, numbness. These are the gifts of the command to look upon God, to look upon the world as it is. Don't blink or turn away. Don't try to fix it. Go ahead and feel your feelings. Compassion is about feeling with another person. You can't be compassionate to others' feeling these emotions unless you get to know them yourself.

June 3, 2004

If that is what God is, then what does it mean to love God?

Throughout my life I have reflected from time to time about what it means to know God, but I'm not sure I have ever posed the question to myself, "What does it mean to love God?"

To love God. Reverence for all things just because they're wonderful. To love God is to love all that is, to wonder at it, to be awestruck by power and complexity and beauty. Even human incompetence is to be held in reverence for the human, the swirl of molecules and impulses, emotions, splendor, and frailty.

That's what it is to love God—to love all the manifestations of Godness. To love them, hold, cherish, honor. Not alter, fix, or judge. To love is to love. Love it all, marvel in it, fall down in reverence to it. Wowie, zowie! Whiz, bang! Gee whiz! Sigh...

Loving God includes resting easy with birth and death, creation and destruction, storm and pestilence, accepting the thorn as part of the flower and the flower as part of the cactus.

To serve God. Service feels different when infused with love. It might include (or exclude) any kind of activity: tender caring, firm rebuking, but infused with love, motivated by love, expressed through love. Serving God includes cultivating compassion, constancy, hope, kindness, generosity, tenderness, clarity, firmness, reliability, humility, simplicity, steadfastness, beauty, power, rhythm, balance.

August 9

I am called to know God in the seaminess of human beings and the works wrought by human hands, in pain and confusion and desperation. I am called to move closer to disorder that I cannot fix and to love the people I find there, perhaps also to have them feel touched by love.

September 5

The way cannot be made straight.

Human nature doesn't change, human struggles remain the same from generation to generation, century to century, millennium to millennium. Is it my lesson to live into my helplessness? Well, yes. I have to live into my helplessness, the way cannot be made straight, not among Quakers, not in electing the right U.S. government, not in forestalling global climate change. What to do will clarify when I accept my helplessness. Love will certainly be part of that doing. Love, respect, reverence.

September 8

This is a hard shift in perspective for me. My lifetime focus has been on the wrinkles that I can smooth.

Love, reverence, respect.

Simplicity, peace, integrity, community, equality: these are attitudes, modes of relationship. Not actions.

October 13

Respect, reverence, love. I'm getting there in theory. That is, when I think about things, interpret things, I am more and more expansive, more ready to keep low, to see various points of view and honor them. But in practice I find myself petulant, angry, controlling, reactive. Am I more emotionally reactive than before or am I noticing it more because of the contrast with how God is inviting me to be?

Love, respect, reverence for myself. Note the emotions as they come up. Honor the vulnerability that contributes to the emotions. Give your vulnerability over to faithfulness. Trust in your deep safety.

October 25

Groundedness is a state of being connected, held, tapped into the source. To be grounded is to surrender to God's power, to surrender to love, respect, and reverence. Grounded is what I need to be consistently loving, reverent and respectful.

One needs to be grounded to be able to tolerate being helpless.

October 28

That's what helplessness is all about: working within an imperfect situation that I can't make right— and doing it with respect, reverence, and love.

November 10

The goal is to have a holy interaction in which both another person and I feel God's presence, then any changes either of us needs to undergo will be in the hands of God's transforming power.

Patricia McBee *is a member of Central Philadelphia Meeting and part of the WCTS editorial team.*

(*What Canst Thou Say?* February 2005
"Loving God with Our Whole Being")

Sunrise on Easter Morning, 2011

Jennifer Elam

New Life amongst
   The daffodils and tulips.
New Life, new calves
   In my Dad's fields.
New Life, lightning flashes,
   thunder roars,
Winds rip apart all in sight;
   tornadoes changing everything
   they touch.
New life, the fires of grief burn
   my soul's forests;
The old is burned and the ground
   made ready for New Life
   emerging.

Tornadoes rip; the tulips just wave
   and pay no mind.

Resurrection…elusive in
   moments…

Yet,
I feel the seedlings,
   Struggling to find the water,
   Struggling to find their
      nourishment;

I hear: stop the busy-ness;
   pay attention to the seedlings.

I feel the abundance, just a
Heartbeat away – so many sources
So much nourishment,
   so many springs—
Ready to wash over me;
Stopped only by my saying—
   not enough YES,
Not enough YES to the water that
   gushes,
Not enough YES to the Love that
   pours forth,
Not enough YES today,
   to the abundance of…it All.

New Life, mine is about learning
   To nourish the seedlings—
More YES, to the wells springing
   forth and gushing engaged
love and Love.

How much YES is possible to the
   Ultimate Love Story?
How much YES is possible to the
   Abundance just waiting?

Jennifer Elam is a member of Berea meeting, Kentucky, but presently attends Swarthmore meeting, Pennsylvania. She is the author of *Dancing with God through The Storm: Mysticism and Mental Illness*. A psychologist who works with children, she is looking forward to guest editing an issue of *WCTS* on Children's Mystical Spirituality.

(*What Canst Thou Say?* August 2011
"Creativity and Mysticism")

April Morning

Helen Weaver Horn

*After dust and drought
a gentle rain. The water
gurgles in the pipes.
Out on the cistern slab
a dove lifts up her wing
and stretches each white
secret underfeather,
catching droplets,
shakes, furls in, lifts up
the other, holds it wide,
the wetness streaming
off her side. Around her
daffodils bow down.*

Helen Weaver Horn is a member of Athens Friends Meeting, OH. She meets monthly with a Quaker Writers & Artists Group. She feels the mystery of Creation in the small daily happenings of the natural world. She and her husband have just incorporated their hill farm as a nature preserve.

(*What Canst Thou Say?* May 2011 "Animals")

Gifts Meant To Be Shared

Sally Campbell

I am so glad that I became a Quaker after Friends came to accept and even appreciate messages that come in the form of song. I read that Herbert Hoover's mother was read out of meeting when she sang her father's favorite hymn at his memorial meeting. (Fortunately another nearby meeting took her in.)

What would I do with these lovely gifts I've been given if I could not sing them in meeting? At FGC Gathering in 1982, I not only found myself saying, "I'll be faithful to you, God, all my life," but I began writing songs, which was a complete surprise. I could not carry a tune, learn the piano or understand musical notation, but here were songs coming out of me. The first one, inspired by a T-shirt with a winking Quaker, was "Hug a Friend."

One day at Morningside Meeting a few years later, a couple of longtime attenders arrived with their new baby, the first child who'd been in the meeting in years. That day the first line of a song was there for me when I sat down, and the whole song was complete in time for me to rise and sing it during meeting. Appropriately it is called, "Give Us This Day a Gentle Song."

In 1990 at FGC Gathering we unfolded sections of the AIDS quilt to honor and grieve so many dear Friends lost to that epidemic. In the deep FLGC worship afterwards, I was comforted by yet another new song, "Elements of Love." It begins "The water of Love will ease us through our grieving" and ends "We will sing new songs of joy. We will lead new lives of peace."

Though these are the three times I felt most clearly that I was given a song in meeting, I have written many more songs over the years and have sung them in and out of meeting. Recently I gave a sermon to Mennonites, telling about my experience of being a Quaker by telling stories and singing some of my songs. I hoped to leave them with one thing I had learned: if we allow it, the Spirit will give us the most wonderful and surprising gifts that are meant to be shared.

I'm so glad Quakers are now open to accepting the gifts of song we have been given. As yet another of my songs says:

> *Rest in the Silence, trust in the Silence*
> *For from the Silence your true song will come*
> *And when you hear it, sing from the Silence*
> *Bring from the Silence the song to be sung*
>
> *Rest in the Spirit, trust in the Spirit*
> *For thanks to the Spirit your song will be sung*
> *And as you sing it, the Spirit sings with you*
> *The song and the Silence and Spirit are one.*

Sally Campbell *is a member of Morningside Meeting, New York City. She is a singer and songwriter and professional organizer of people's stuff.*

(*What Canst Thou Say?* November 2010 "Silence and Music")

Worshipful Vision

Zarinea Lee Zolivea

Observe blue black shadows whispering a quiet reverence
Experience the thunderous cloudbursts before the purple storm
Listen attentively to screaming violent wind
Dare to bear bitter icy cold winters
Smell spring's misty rose petals
Savor sweltering hot summers
Recall sweet gardens of elaborate beauty
Relish the autumn equinox of stupendous colors
Flood mother sky with worshipful vision
Stroll along the foaming waves of the oceanfront
Feel the cool raindrops upon your skin
Perceive luscious moons
Revel in the glory of the rainbow
Love the birthing process of wondrous creation
Chant the symphony of the forest while picturing music in eternity
Use life like a delirious goddess singing a delicate dream.

Zarinea Lee Zolivea is a literacy teacher, and a writer of poems and short articles.

(*What Canst Thou Say?* November 2007
"Feminine Aspects of the Divine")

As I Have Showed You
James Baker

At a time of deep searching

Suddenly

There He was.

Stand up—You are in the Presence of the Risen Christ.

The most male of beings

yet the most female of awarenesses

I looked deeply into His eyes

and I know now what compassion is

and unconditional Love.

Wordlessly I asked Him questions

about my family, myself.

His answers surprising,

accurate, years later.

The experience decades ago

still fresh as yesterday—

of the reality of his touch,

The Presence of His Being

the understood imperative;

Go and love others

as I have showed you by My life—

There are no words sufficient….

James Arnold Baker has retired and returned home to his family, especially to be with and help his youngest son and three littlest grandchildren in Nelson, British Columbia. He retains his membership in Downers Grove Meeting, Illinois.

(*What Canst Thou Say?* August 2006 "Jesus")

Getting Real with God

Jennifer Elam

I had finished graduate school only the year before and was a temporary assistant professor at the university where I had gotten my master's degree. It was going quite badly.

My ex-professors turned colleagues could not make the switch, and I was devastated. I was living on campus, and one day I was home and very sad. I was crying, wailing actually. And I started screaming at God. Being a person taught to fear God and be polite and please everyone, I never before had considered doing such a thing and actually did not consider it that day. It just happened.

I screamed at God for hours. I knew no one was home next door, but suddenly there was a knock on the door. I asked, "Who are you and what do you want?" It was the campus plumbers coming to fix something I had asked them to fix weeks prior. I told them to come in at their own risk, because I was quite upset with God and was busy yelling at God at the moment. They started laughing and told me to give God a couple for them too.

They soon left and I continued to yell and scream and cry. I had had it. After about two hours, I suddenly got very calm and heard a soft, gentle voice say,

"It's about time you got more real with me. I can take whatever you have to give me."

Alone in my apartment, I was startled to hear the voice that was not mine. An image of God smiling came to me.

My relationship with God changed that day. It was forever to be different. Many times since then when I have been upset and fretting (about nothing worth fretting about), I have gotten an image of God having a belly laugh. And God's belly laugh always puts things in better perspective!

Jennifer Elam *is the author of* Dancing with God through the Storm: Mysticism and Mental Illness.

(*What Canst Thou Say?* November 2005 "God's Humor")

Blessings Beyond Naming

Christine O'Brien

*Precious inner teacher
Love that guides me,
My heart is open.
All of creation is my blessing,
Calling me to love.
I rest in what is.
My imperfections teach me tolerance and forgiveness.
Inner teacher, guide me.
Heal my heart.
Heal my ways.
I rest in blessings beyond naming,
Always.*

Christine O'Brien is a member of the St. Petersburg Meeting and is working on the 35th year of Circus McGurkis: the People's Fair, whose theme this year is "People Make Change: Rosa Parks Memorial Circus McGurkis."

(*What Canst Thou Say?* May 2006 "Changed by Grace")

~~~~~~~~~~~

Ice in Someone Else's Soup

Judy Lumb

I dream that I am sitting at a lunch counter eating soup with a friend. I decide my soup is too hot, so I put ice in it. Then I reach over to put ice in my friend's soup, when the booming voice of God comes from behind me, *"You can't put ice in someone else's soup!"* Every time I start to meddle in someone else's life, I hear the booming voice of God saying, *"You can't put ice in someone else's soup!"*

Judy Lumb *is a member of Atlanta (Georgia) Friends Meeting, but lives in Caye Caulker, Belize, Central America.*

(*What Canst Thou Say?* November 2005 "God's Humor")

Bat Line to God

Lauren Leach

I had a Catholic up-bringing. I thought the confessionals were elevators and the office phone in the rectory was the Bat Line to God. You know that little box in the front of the church with the red candle hanging in front of it? That's where the host was kept. The little red candle was a nightlight to keep Jesus company. The priest always said the host wasn't really Jesus until he said those prayers during Mass, but if not, why did they have to keep a nightlight on in front of the host box? So, it was Jesus in there, but we weren't really cannibals during Communion because it was more like a piece of Jesus's soul was in each of those little pieces of bread. Besides, we weren't eating it, we were swallowing it—like medicine, which of course isn't really food either because you can take medicine one hour before Communion, but you can't eat. You didn't want to chew the host—you had to swallow it before it got stuck to the roof of your mouth—because then you'd be a cannibal. And if you ate one hour before Communion, then Jesus' soul wouldn't get into your bloodstream.

Lauren Leach *is a member of Urbana-Champaign (Illinois) Meeting, currently living in Maryville, Missouri.*

(*What Canst Thou Say?* November 2005 "God's Humor")

Nooks and Crannies

Mariellen Gilpin

While my evening prayers are certainly heartfelt and constantly evolving, they can also be rote. Part of my standard prayer is to thank God for helping us accept God's friendship and companionship "in every nook and cranny of life." One night I was very tired and rushed through my prayers, trying to get them all said before my medication put me to sleep. I paraphrased, in order to get the gist without dwelling on the word choices so much as to slow me down. I left out the "nooks and crannies" phrase, and instantly there was a Voice speaking in tones of mock aggrievement,

"What, no nooks and crannies?"

That woke me up!

Mariellen Gilpin *celebrates the many ways God has helped her deal with mental illness.*

(*What Canst Thou Say?* November 2005 "God's Humor")

Horny for God

Mariellen Gilpin

For almost 30 years, when I had sexual thoughts, I connected them with the name of a sexual abuser and the memories of the abuse and resultant shame. Finally in 2006, I had resolved the memories, which were symptoms of Post Traumatic Stress Disorder (PTSD), and come to a place of objective compassion about the abuser—I simply didn't need the PTSD symptoms anymore. All I had left after 2006 was the abuser's name. I habitually repeated it in two contexts, only: upon first awakening in the morning, before I was even fully conscious, and also whenever I remembered any time I'd been shamed as a child as much as 50 or 60 years before.

Those childhood shames had not necessarily been sexual. I remember, for instance, being blamed because I'd sat on the bench at my piano recital in such a way that my mother's red bias binding on the hem of my homemade pink dress showed—horrors! As Amy Perry says, "Shame is an acronym meaning Should Have Already Mastered Everything." So, between 2006 and 2009, I continued working and praying to stop saying the abuser's name. I wanted no remaining triggers that might sometime lead me down that *name-sexual thoughts-memories-shame* primrose path again.

So, in May of 2009, a few months after the gift of praying in healing was restored to me, some of us agreed to pray for a friend while she had a very serious eye operation. We would pray the entire time of the surgery—four hours. We started on time, but the surgeon did not, so instead of praying for four hours, we prayed for six. Our friend recovered nicely. The next morning when I first woke up, I said God's name. The shame-response simply hasn't happened in that context ever again.

I've continued working and praying with redoubled vigor about that other shame-response. The prayer basically boiled down to "Let thy name be the one on my lips" (in the moment of remembering my old shame). Having a sexual response during prayer was so not a part of my culture growing up, but it began to happen to me. I wish I would have been able to trust someone wise enough to talk about it 35 years ago. That someone might have said, "Honey, you're just horny for God!"

The idea never occurred to me. I had read John of the Cross in college, but I thought that sex stuff was just a metaphor. I read *Song of Solomon* in various Bible literature classes, and I noticed my professors didn't know quite what to make of it, and moved on to safer territory. My actual experiences 35 years ago sent me down a long, long detour. Finally in 2010, I suddenly felt madly in love with God.

Intimacy with God

One Tuesday in May, 2011, in the midst of a unitive experience, the prayer came from my gut: "Let thy name be the one on my lips!" The prayer was no different, just different in the depth of feeling.

My experience has been that prayers from the gut are extremely powerful. Something wonderful will happen. It may not be precisely what I've asked for, or on my timetable, but God answers that kind of prayer.

The following Tuesday at my semi-annual session with my counselor I told her about the prayer. I went on to say, "The shame-response has been happening less often in recent months. I figure, if I go two weeks without making the shame-response, it's time to declare a miracle." My therapist agreed wholeheartedly, yes, two weeks meant I was healed.

The following Tuesday was an intensely busy day. I was in the midst of solving some complicated problem that took my entire focus—and suddenly I realized it had been two weeks. I was healed. My level of intensity doubled in about a second and a half. My joy was huge, just huge.

And then...on Day Eighteen, the shame-response happened again. Not so fast, Mariellen. But how can I feel shame about being a sexual being when God is my lover?

I was okay about the 18-day mistake because 18 days was a pretty great record. I would just continue praying, working, and being madly in love with God. Being horny for God.

Then I woke up and the first words out of my mouth were, "My Love." God has decided what Name he wants me to call him, first thing in the morning. Increasingly that remembered shame has been met with, "My Love." A couple of weeks ago, I remembered something I did 50 years ago about which I jolly well should feel shame. Unbidden out of my mouth came, "How sad," not the unhealthy shame-response—as if, deep inside, I've forgiven myself for being human, being sexual. It's like those mystic guys say, "Keep your focus on God. All the rest will fall away."

Mariellen Gilpin is the Coordinator and the heart and soul of What Canst Thou Say?

(*What Canst Thou Say?* February 2012 "Shame")

Icon

Kathleen Maia Tapp

When you came into my dreams
   you wore a guise of chocolate
      and so, I knew you not.

First, a chocolate curtain
   of intricate design;

I wondered idly
    what lay beyond,
      felt vague yearnings...

Then a tall woman appeared,
    rich dark milk spilling
      from her breasts.

One morning
   before dawn I drifted
      into a light sleep,
and saw a goddess
    made of chocolate.

And then I knew.
About the chocolate.
How it spoke of unknown realms
   rich, deep,
      mysterious...

This chocolate, sweet talisman
    dark icon,
tossed from the night shores—
a sign of your veiled presence,
   O Black Madonna.

Kathleen Maia Tapp is a former editor of WCTS. She travels all over the world, seeking out holy places.

(*What Canst Thou Say?* November 2007
"Feminine Aspects of the Divine")

Intimacy with God

In the Land of the Great Mother

Kathleen Maia Tapp

I followed the huge throng of passengers crossing the Mexico City airport. Speaking only a few words of Spanish, I was nervous to be traveling alone to Mexico. A huge wave of relief washed over me to see a woman standing near the exit, as promised, holding out a sign that said "GATE."*

Over the next 10 days, by bus, subway, taxi and on foot, we visited many ancient sites of the Great Mother in the central highlands of Mexico. Our guide was Cecilia Corcoran, a Franciscan nun who did her doctoral research among the ruins, following the trail of the goddess through the many layers of history. We visited the circular pyramid of San Cuicuilco, the oldest ceremonial site in the Valley of Mexico. We walked the spiral path to the top, where a sanctuary has been unearthed. The sun was hot, the atmosphere calm and peaceful, even though the site is completely hemmed in by modern high rise buildings. Many female figures have been found here.

At Teotihuacán, we learned the story of Chalchiuhtlicue—Goddess of the Flowing Waters. Her thirteen foot high stone statue reveals a well developed head and torso, with her lower body undeveloped as it blends into the earth, like a mountain. It is said that on the day she was moved to the Museum of Anthropology, there were huge storms.

We visited Tepeyec, where the Virgin of Guadalupe appeared to a Nahuatl man named Juan Diego in 1531. She appeared at the same spot where the Aztec goddess Tonantsin had long been worshipped. Juan Diego's cloak, imprinted with the Lady's image is hanging on the basilica wall and viewed by millions of pilgrims each year. In Nahuatl language, she was known as "She Who Comes Flying from the Lake Like an Eagle of Fire" and "Mother of the True God; Mother of the Giver of Life; Mother of Heaven and Earth."

I had felt a gentle summons in dreams and other nudgings to take this pilgrimage—especially to Tepeyec. I knew it would take time for me to integrate it all—the vast sweep of history and the Presence evidenced in so many ways, both at these ancient sites we visited and at places where modern women were hard at work establishing low cost clinics, agencies to help victims of domestic violence, and women's cooperatives.

And over a year later, the pilgrimage to Mexico is still imparting its grace. As world events spiral ever more alarmingly toward unrest and violence, I remember the words that the Virgin at Guadalupe spoke to Juan Diego, at

---

*Global Awareness Through Experience (GATE) also sponsors women's spiritual quests to the sites of the Black Madonna in Europe, and other pilgrimages. <www GATE-Travel.org>.

a time of great destruction when his world was being totally altered by the Spanish conquest:

"Do you not know that I am your mother?—Do not be troubled or disturbed.—Is there anything else you need?"

Kathleen Maia Tapp *is a former editor of WCTS. She travels all over the world, seeking out holy places.*

(*What Canst Thou Say?* November 2007
"Feminine Aspects of the Divine")

Photography as Gratitude
Allison Randall

I was brought up to be grateful. My parents didn't set out to teach me gratefulness, but they modeled it almost every day of my life. At home, when there was a snowstorm or it was autumn or there were birds at the feeder or a cardinal in a tree, they would bring our attention to it, commenting on its beauty with awe in their voices.

For most of my life, gratitude has sprung freely from my heart. When I see a sunset, I feel grateful. When I look at one of my children or grandchildren, I feel great gratitude. When I see a birch tree, a beautiful rock, a kind face in the grocery store, the light through green leaves, when my car starts up easily on a cold morning, or I hear the voice of a friend on the phone, when I eat blueberries or strawberries or even just my morning cereal, when I hear Beethoven, or hold the hand of my husband or my granddaughter, my heart fills immediately with gratitude. So many moments in every day are short and heart-sprung wordless prayers of gratitude.

For a particular section of time in my life, however, gratitude was more difficult. After an incident of sexual abuse 11 1/2 years ago, my heart quickly threw up a protective shell around it which was very useful for keeping men out, very effective in making me feel safe, but that shell also kept out gratitude. My world became much smaller, and my heart did too. A heart that is not full of gratitude shrinks like a deflated balloon, and feels just as flat.

The world seemed too dangerous a place to be open to in the way I had been accustomed to. Those days of heavy Post Traumatic Stress Disorder (PTSD) were overwhelming. I could clear only one dish at a time off my table, I could cut out and sew up only one cloth toy at a time, could read only one and a half pages of a book at a sitting, could face only one task of any sort at a time, and even that was frequently too much. I avoided the grocery store or anywhere there were a lot of people, I moved into a basement apartment so there wasn't too much to see out the windows. The world was too big a place to take in all at once. I had to keep my world small.

About six months after the abuse, one of my brothers gave me a camera that was remarkably easy to use. A camera that thought for me, because I couldn't think much for myself during those dark days. The camera had a zoom feature so I could see things close up. Instead of looking at a whole forest or even one tree, I could put the camera protectively up to my face, zoom in and concentrate on one burl on one tree. Instead of seeing the whole sky I could see one cloud formation. Looking through the lens was safe: it kept the world small enough for me not to be afraid, and I discovered that these small frames of the world were beautiful. And in seeing the beauty I felt grateful. Each time I put the camera to my eye and framed a small piece of nature I felt gratitude. Each time I held one of my photographs, a rectangle of paper that was a small piece of the world, a close up manageable and beautiful piece, I felt gratitude. Each photograph I took became a prayer of gratefulness.

Since my gratitude has always been to God, whom I consider to be responsible for all the beauty and goodness and deliciousness in the world, when my heart had been full of gratitude and full of prayers it was full of God. And when my heart had shrunk and was protected by a shell, it could only let in a little gratitude at a time, a little God at a time. But that camera helped me extend my vision. Through the eye of that camera I could peek out at the world as if through a small hole in my shell, and I came to learn that God was indeed still out there in the larger world, as well as hidden away in my heart. And I was hugely grateful.

Through much photography, prayer, counseling, prayer, journaling, prayer, sewing, and Grace, the larger world is no longer unreasonably frightening to me. I still struggle with PTSD on and off, but am no longer overwhelmed by it. I continue to take photographs, and most of them are close-ups rather than large scenes; I became very partial to that scope and consider those photographs to be closely focused prayers. Gratefulness-prayer photography has become part of my day-to-day life, one of my spiritual practices, a way of translating the mystical experience of heart-striking awed gratitude into picture form.

Allison Randall is a member of Keene, New Hampshire, Friends Meeting, and attempts to stay open to The Divine.

(*What Canst Thou Say?* August 2009 "Body Prayer")

My Golden Pond

Patricia Reitemeyer

I was teaching, keeping house, single, caring for my children alone, and working on my dissertation. I was lonely, greatly overworked, and had become very depressed. My responsibilities were overwhelming, life was simply terrible, and I was frightened of both the present and the future.

But my friend was determined to persevere, so we spread out our towels on the beach. I went in the water, although with some distaste for its murky condition. To avoid the crowd I went out beyond the ropes to where it was so deep I could do a strong swim. I swam awhile and it felt good. As I started to wade back toward the beach, a young boy stood up in the water a few feet before me, and laughing, yelled, "Hey, lady!" and threw a beach ball toward me. I was going to ignore him and the ball, when for some reason I reached out and caught it instead.

As soon as I did, the water began to shine and mysteriously turn gold—a deep, beautiful gold. Immediately my analyzing brain reported that the gold was a reflection of oil on the water's surface. Surely.

I was in no mood to play, but I did throw the ball back to the boy. As it went through the air, it shone with surprising golden outlines. The boy caught it and laughed—and as he did, his dark brown skin began to glow golden. He looked stunningly beautiful. I was overwhelmed and stood paralyzed in the water for a moment. Then I turned, much puzzled, and looked around to the other people, to the beach, the shore, the trees beyond, and all, all of it, was a beautiful glowing gold, the whole landscape, even every leaf. A soft, soft gold. I held my breath, transfixed, as I stood in the water. I could hardly believe my eyes. It was beautiful beyond description.

Then the boy threw the ball at me again, and as I looked at him, all golden, I saw him for what he was: a strong, joyful, beautiful, shining young spirit. I picked the ball out of the water and threw it back to him. Then in some unfathomable way I knew that he and all the other golden people on the golden beach were my people, and I was theirs. No separation of race or culture. We were all, every one, united in an enveloping, ethereal, golden glow.

After a moment of trying vainly to understand, and then quickly seeing that I couldn't, I began walking slowly into the glow. I felt transformed. But as I approached the shore the golden glow retreated before me and began to fade. I tried to hold onto it, but couldn't. By the time I got back to our place on the beach and my friend, it had disappeared. I sat down on my towel in a daze, and she looked at me, puzzled, and asked what had happened. I couldn't tell her, couldn't find words. How explain to her that I had seen the world and all of us within it as it really is: somehow gloriously enfolded together in gold! I couldn't talk about it. I just knew I'd seen something from another reality. I knew I had been graced with a vision.

After a few minutes, for no logical reason, I saw that my miserable life was not only actually okay but in reality was very, very good. The heavy depression that had plagued me for months was gone! I felt protected, reassured, even loved.

The depression came back a little as the days wore on, but I held on to the fact that the reality we live in isn't limited by our three-dimensional world, that there is another dimension entirely that interpenetrates, in which all is well, all is golden, all people are connected and glow with the Spirit within. I had literally seen it. There was no need for worry. None at all.

__Patricia Reitemeyer__ has studied metaphysics for 40 years, and practiced religions east and west. "There is so much more to consciousness than we can ever hope to know or, indeed, experience—but I keep trying." She attends Bloomington Friends Meeting, Indiana.

(*What Canst Thou Say?* May 2007 "Unseen Hands")

Worship

Michael Resman

*Closing my eyes
I rest in the arms of the
Lord.
Quiet settles
stirred by the rustling of angels.*

*Expectant silence
waits to hear again
the word of God.
In community
celebrating
this taste of heaven.*

Michael Resman recently retired because he felt called to a new career—praying. He spends hours each day in prayer activities: silent prayer, walking in parks, and cross stitching children's clothing for a homeless shelter. In order to leave adequate time for prayer, he has avoided taking on other tasks. He continues to follow a long-term call to write. He is Clerk of Rochester, Minnesota, Friends Meeting.

(*What Canst Thou Say?* November 2008 "Angels")

Drenched with Love
Vera Dickinson

At 33 years old, I was married to a good husband, had three healthy children, friends, a lovely home and was involved in community affairs. I should have felt successful and happy. Instead, internally I was dust and ashes. Nothing gave me joy.

I decided there were too many years ahead of me to continue in this gray way. What was missing? Was it this "God" which so far I had managed so well without? While pegging out the clothes I decided that something did exist, and I'd go for it. I bought a book on the subject but found it was of no help. However, my inner yearning day and night was very real.

One morning I woke up and felt full of energy and very well. All of my senses were keener—colours, smells, hearing—all of nature radiantly surrounded me. I laughed and said, "For goodness sake, I've been sickening for something all these months and now I've thrown it off—it's wonderful." At this time Lynn, my 7 year old, was hurried into hospital for an emergency appendix operation. It turned out that the ailment was not the appendix, but doctors couldn't say what it was. I visited the hospital daily, and she was very ill. It puzzled me that I was not worried but completely at peace. Deeply within I knew that if she lived all was well, and if she died all would be well, that underneath were the everlasting arms. I thought to myself that I must have seen this last bit on some church billboard.

Almost a month went by and one day, after visiting Lynn who lay thin and white with a brown liquid oozing from the corner of her mouth, peace left me. When I arrived home I crossed the bedroom floor for a weep on the bed. As I did so, a stern voice said to me, "You haven't enough faith." My next thought was that the word "faith" was not part of my vocabulary. Could this be God who was talking to me? As I stood there, it was as if I was being drenched like the time I washed my hair under a waterfall, but this drenching wasn't water, it was love. And every person who lived was being drenched with love like this all the time. I had found God! No, God was making himself known to me—God had been there all the time.

For some time afterwards I found it difficult to just walk when going down the street—I wanted to dance and skip. I wanted to find high buildings and shout from their rooftops, "I love God and God loves me!" I was running over with joy. Lynn recovered shortly afterwards.

My life changed. It became full of meaning—everything I did was for God. I felt very tender to all and sundry, and became interested in everyone I met. I also knew that I didn't have to help everyone—only those who came within my orbit. My health improved, and I had boundless energy. An inner heavy dragging sensation vanished. I felt released from The World and its values, and oh what a relief that was. I felt more "at home" in the world at the same time, and lost some of my fear of the sea. Creepy crawly things became more friendly—although some of the dislike of these has returned over the years. Time seemed able to stretch. There was a neighbour and two friends whom I divined had ailments, and these could be cured if they had Faith. I could tell when a minister spoke what his inner condition was regarding God. This state of inwardly knowing others lasted for about ten weeks which I have since regarded as being in a state of grace.

I began to read the Bible and books with a spiritual content. One night I was sitting up in bed reading a book written by a psychiatrist who was treating his patients by faith. One of his patients had rheumatism. I was wearing what I had been using since teen-age, padded sleeves on my upper arms to keep warm as I had rheumatism there. I said to myself, "I've got rheumatism, and it can be helped by faith. Well I've got enough of that." I threw the pads into the waste-paper basket in the corner. As I did so a light seemed to shine inside of me, and I raised my arms above my head—something I hadn't been able to do since I was 14.

I lived in this joyful state for almost a year. I had the sensation of a helpful presence always being just behind my right shoulder. But one day I felt a little niggle of bad temper. This was so unpleasant— as if I'd been walking in heaven and one leg had gone through into hell. I didn't want this to happen again. I determined to look for a group of people who had the same sort of experience as me and find out what they did. I first approached a chemistry teacher friend of ours who was about to become a Baptist minister, and told him my story asking to be steered to a God-minded group. He explained that my body had had its chemistry upturned, but it wasn't something to be worried about, it would pass and all would be well. So I went to the Presbyterian Minister in town and told him my story, asking to join the group in his church who had had similar experiences. He told me that such a group didn't exist in his church, that I was a young and impressionable woman with a temperament which was changeable, and that this would settle down with maturity. Increasingly amazed I made the rounds of various church services in town and drew a blank.

Finally my husband suggested that I look up the Quakers. I hit the day of their Monthly Meeting, but as I liked what I had experienced I asked to stay on for the business meeting, too. At the end of their meeting I was offered the London book of Christian Faith and Practice in the Experience of Friends. There at the beginning were the accounts of people who had had similar experiences to mine. I had found my group!

The direction of my life and family changed. Once I became God-centred I welcomed difficult work presented to me. It was an opportunity for showing my love. Fortunately I have a husband willing to be supportive enough to undergo the changes of home, jobs and activities and even the introduction into our home of difficult personalities for months or even years. The "presence" lasted many years, but finally faded away. I grieved about this at first, until realizing I was now out of kindergarten and operating on my own. We look back with wonder and pleasure on the variety and interest of it all—and it is still continuing. Now 80 years old next year, I find the thought of death holds no sting. That of God in me will go back to God. Joy!

Vera Dickinson lives in Motueka, New Zealand. She writes that "your little magazine [WCTS] is filling a present gap for me in the N.Z. Quaker scene at present."
(*What Canst Thou Say?* February 2005
"Loving God with our Whole Being")

I Give Thanks
Janet Means Underhill

The candles held us in the soft light out of the surrounding darkness. I was seated about five feet from a Russian icon of the face of Jesus. It had not been my intention to be there. Tilden Edwards, then director of the Shalem Institute for Spiritual Formation, had invited participants to join in an evening presentation of Russian icons.

My response had been negative. Why would I, a Quaker, want to sit with icons? A dear friend was deeply fed spiritually by icons. I had attempted to use them, but they never spoke to me. All day my will struggled with an inner voice and palpable energy which kept nudging me to attend. In my usual resistant, heels-digging-ruts-into-the-carpet fashion, I entered the darkened room. There were four icons on easels in the front. I was drawn to sit facing the face of Jesus.

The soft glow of the candles and reverence of the setting held us as we went into silence. Tilden spoke softly, then left us to be with the Mystery. We were in a covered meeting.

As I sat with the Presence, I was moved to look at the face of Jesus. His gaze became alive. I was drawn into his compassionate eyes. He reached his hand through my body and held my heart. I could see my heart. It was the shape and texture of a rough, hard geode. I was amazed to realize my heart was so hardened. Jesus and I sat together with me held in his loving gaze and him gently holding my heart. Warmth began to flow through me. My heart broke in two, revealing a shimmering crystal interior. My tears flowed. Wounds were healed. I give thanks.

Janet Means Underhill *is a member of Lake Forest Meeting, Illinois, and a longtime member of Illinois Yearly Meeting's Ministry and Advancement Committee.*
(*What Canst Thou Say?* August 2006 "Jesus")

▶ *Intimacy with God*

Mystery and Wonder Fill My World
For These I Am Grateful

Janet Means Underhill

Have you seen dawn rising to greet the sun?
Have you gazed at the stars filling the dome of sky on a dark night?
Have you watched a spider drop into unknown space
 and weave his web?

Mystery and Wonder fill my world

Do you greet the smiles of strangers passing on the streets?
Do you feel the touch of another's hand?
Do you sink into Silence and let yourself be held by The Other?

Mystery and Wonder fill my world

When the world turns dark and fearful,
When you are consumed by despair and grief,
When there seems no hope or reason,
When you have tripped over your frailties—again,

Have you expanded into the hammock of love and safety
 that undergirds you?
Have you known it is not you who makes the rules and leads the way?

In the absence of all comes The All,
Your world turns,
You are breathed into life
To move forward.

Mystery and Wonder fill my world
For these I am grateful.

Janet Means Underhill is a member of Lake Forest Meeting, Illinois. She is a member of Illinois Yearly Meeting's Ministry and Advancement committee.

(*What Canst Thou Say?* February 2009 "Gratefulness")

Author Index

Adams, Alicia, 111
Adams, Joyce B., 144
Ansell, Janis, 87, 88
Arbiter, Robin, 100
Ashurst, Rhonda, 134
Bagus, Eileen, 69
Baker, James, 60, 163
Barnes, Bob, 154
Blair, David, 27
Blanchard, Rosemary, 66
Blocher, Heidi, 78
Bruce, Carmen, 7
Campbell, Sally, 160
Clearbridge, Barbara, 85
De Sa, Elizabeth, 45
Dickinson, Vera, 175
Elam, Jennifer, 137, 159, 164
Favor, Judith, 141
Ferguson, Janet, 139
Fitz, Phil, 54
Frick, Jennifer, 96
Geiger, Wendy Clarissa, 97
Gilpin, Mariellen, 65, 166, 167
Glazer, Mary Kay, 77
Gordon, Elizabeth K., 41
Hannah, JZW, 112
Harper, Robin W., 51
Hawkins, Viv, 82
Heldreth, Lillian, 15, 152
Herzog, Diann, 148
Highland, Anne, 74, 115
Hillman, Gene, 16
Hopkins, Mary R., 9
Horn, Helen Weaver, 19, 160
Jacobsen, Katharine, 30
Jarman, Roswitha, 4
Jones, Marcia J., 150
Jonjak, Hazel, 23, 145
Kimball, Jeanne, 80
Kirby, Lynn, 117
Krueger, Charleen, 8, 138
Leach, Lauren, 166
Lee, Linda Caldwell, 73
Lumb, Glynis, 35

Lumb, Judy, 49, 165
Martin, Marcelle, 29
McBee, Patricia, 155
McDougall, Erin, 47
Melick, Pam, 75
Miranda-Feliciano, Evelyn, 130
Mittenthal, Jay, 68
Morton, Peg, 57
Mueller, William H., 146
Neidigh, Verna (Marty), 71, 146
O'Brien, Christine, 37, 165
Paulsen, Faith, 34, 91
Perry, Amy, 14
Pfaltzgraff-Carlson, Rhonda, 62, 124
Pomeroy, Lois, 26
Povolny, Joyce, 33
Pyle, Maurine, 13, 61
Rada, Lee, 102
Randall, Allison, 101, 171
Reeks, Angeline, 114
Reitemeyer, Patricia, 173
Resman, Michael, 39, 115, 174
Roberts, Dalton, 11, 105
Roberts, Jean, 89
Roth, Carol, 94, 106
Sabelman, Eric, 84
Satterfield, Mary, 133
Scherer, Anne, 128
Schobernd, Beth, 123
Schobernd, Paul, 118
Shaw, Deborah L., 129
Siciliano, Helen, 142
Stanford, Merry, 5
Stillwell, Ruth, 90
Tapp, Kathleen Maia, 53, 169, 170
Theresa, Linda, 17, 140
Treadway, Carolyn Wilbur, 126
Tucker, Laurie, 20
Underhill, Janet Means, 177, 178
Vernon, Sadie, 149
Waddington, Mary, 21
Waisvisz, Cathy, 110
Zolivea, Zarinea Lee, 40, 162

Past Issues of What Canst Thou Say?

Why Canst Thou Say? Is a newsletter in which Quakers share first-hand their mystical experiences and contemplative practice. The first fourteen issues were published from October 1994 through May 1997. Each issue featured a variety of topics. Beginning with issue 15 in August 1997, the publication became quarterly, with each issue focusing on a specific theme:

Letting Your Life Speak, August 1997 (15)
Support for the Journey, November 1997 (16)
Deepening Worship and Ministry, February 1998 (17)
Healing, May 1998 (18)
Discernment, August 1998 (19)
Mentors, Mentoring, November 1998 (20)
Nature, February 1999 (21)
Dreams, May 1999 (22)
Speaking Out About Our Mystical Experiences, August 1999 (23)
Mystical Experiences in Childhood, November 1999 (24)
Wholeness in the Midst of Brokenness, February 2000 (25)
Traditions that Feed My Soul, May 2000 (26)
Called to Intercessory Prayer, August 2000 (27)
Visions and Voices, November 2000 (28)
Experiencing the Spirit in Quaker Business Process, February 2001 (29)
Solitude, May 2001 (30)
Forgiving, August 2001 (31)
Kundalini Energy, November 2001 (32)
Spiritual Experience and the Outward Life, February 2002 (33)
The Arts and the Spirit, May 2002 (34)
God's Marvelous Workarounds, August 2002 (35)
Spiritual Metaphors, November 2002 (36)
Death and Dying, February 2003 (37)
Birth and Rebirth, May 2003 (38)
Celebration and Thanksgiving, August 2003 (39)
Spiritual Healing, November 2003 (40)
Open and Tender, February 2004 (41)
Guidance, May 2004 (42)
Knowings, August 2004 (43)
Darkness, November 2004 (44)
Loving God with Our Whole Being, February 2005 (45)
Spiritual Emergence(y), May 2005 (46)
Seeing, August 2005 (47)
God's Humor, November 2005 (48)
Touched by the Spirit, February 2006 (49)
Changed by Grace, May 2006 (50)
Jesus, August 2006 (51)
Evil, November 2006 (52)
Spirituality in the Workplace, February 2007 (53)
Unseen Hands, May 2007 (54)
Hospitality, August 2007 (55)
Feminine Aspects of the Divine, November 2007 (56)
Called, February 2008 (57)
Transforming Conflicts, May 2008 (58)
Telepathy, August 2008 (59)
Angels, November 2008 (60)
Gratefulness, February 2009 (61)
Strangers, May 2009 (62)
Body Prayer, August 2009 (63)
Bread and Roses, November 2009 (64)
A Covenant with Creation, February 2010 (65)
Addiction and Grace, May 2010 (66)
Questioning, August 2010 (67)
Silence and Music, November 2010 (68)
Prayer, February 2011 (69)
Animals, May 2011 (70)
Creativity and Mysticism, August 2011 (71)
Death and Dying, November 2011 (72)
Shame, February 2012 (73)
Disabilities, June 2012 (74)
Unity, August 2012 (75)
Children's Mystical Experiences, November 2012 (76)
Prophetic Vision, February 2013 (77)
Meaning from Despair, May 2013 (78)
Literature as Revelation, August 2013 (79)
Trials and Temptations, November 2013 (80)Past
Spirit-Led Writing, February 2014 (81)
Holding On and Letting Go, May 2014 (82)
Sacred Places, August 2013 (83)
Religious Wounding, November 2014 (84)

To subscribe or purchase copies of back issues of What Canst Thou Say?, see <whatcanstthousay.org>.

In Memoriam

Eileen Bagus

Janet Ferguson

Anne Highland

Evelyn Miranda-Feliciano

Marty Neidigh

Christine O'Brien

Paul Schobernd

Ruth Stillwell

Linda Theresa

Janet Means Underhill

Sadie Vernon

Thanks to these regular authors of *What Canst Thou Say* who have passed on to the next life. They have shared some of their most precious experiences with this worship-sharing community. Their stories have encouraged us all. May we meet them someday, face to face, and celebrate our reunion.

www.ingramcontent.com/pod-product-compliance
Lightning Source LLC
Chambersburg PA
CBHW071202160426
43196CB00011B/2170